CURRICULUM HANDBOOK
FOR
PARENTS AND TEACHERS

ABOUT THE AUTHOR

Doctor Carpenter has taught and served as an administrator in both urban and suburban public school systems
in New York and New Jersey since 1947. She retired in
1984 after spending ten years as a Superintendent of
Schools. Now she devotes her full time to writing. She
earned her Ph.D. at New York University in 1973 and
graduated with a Founder's Day Award. She has been
listed for many years in *Who's Who of American Women.*

CURRICULUM HANDBOOK FOR PARENTS AND TEACHERS

What We Ought to Find Happening in the Public School Classrooms of America

By

BETTY O. CARPENTER, Ph.D.

CHARLES C THOMAS • PUBLISHER
Springfield • Illinois • U.S.A.

Published and Distributed Throughout the World by

CHARLES C THOMAS • PUBLISHER
2600 South First Street
Springfield, Illinois 62794-9265

© *1991 by* CHARLES C THOMAS • PUBLISHER

ISBN 0-398-05719-2

Library of Congress Catalog Card Number: 90-48505

With THOMAS BOOKS *careful attention is given to all details of manufacturing
and design. It is the Publisher's desire to present books that are satisfactory as to
their physical qualities and artistic possibilities and appropriate for their particular
use.* THOMAS BOOKS *will be true to those laws of quality that assure a good
name and good will.*

Printed in the United States of America
SC-R-3

Library of Congress Cataloging-in-Publication Data

Carpenter, Betty O.
    Curriculum handbook for parents and teachers : what we ought to
find happening in the public school classrooms of America / by Betty
O. Carpenter.
      p. cm.
    Includes bibliographical references and index.
    ISBN 0-398-05719-2 (alk. paper)
    1. Education—United States—Curricula. I. Title.
LB1570. C262 1991
375'.00973—dc20
                                            90-48505
                                               CIP

PREFACE

Throughout my lengthy and multifaceted career as a teacher and administrator in the American public schools, I was repeatedly asked by parents for something that would tell them what their children were supposed to be learning in their classes that year. I knew my colleagues were being asked the same question. I am certain that, today, parents still have the same need to know.

I always wondered why there was so little available which would give both parents and educators a handy reference to the scope and sequence of what we offer in our classrooms, especially since what is taught in American public schools is so similar all over the country.

I began teaching in public elementary schools in 1947. In the years since, I have been a classroom teacher, a school vice-principal, an acting principal, a teacher trainer, a central office personnel administrator, a contract negotiator, an adjunct professor, an assistant superintendent of schools, and, for the ten years prior to my recent retirement, a superintendent of schools in a kindergarten through grade twelve public school district.

Through all these years and in all these positions, I have had an intense interest in curriculum and have worked with many educators in an effort to describe it intelligibly. What makes this difficult is that there is a gray area between the "what" and the "how" of the educational process. By focusing on the content itself, rather than on how the content is presented or embellished by the teacher, it became possible to develop this guide.

The goal was to be succinct and at the same time to offer a maximum of information concerning the kind of knowledge and the range of skills students should be achieving in each grade and subject class, and to make this information available to the population at large, as well as to the classroom teacher, for whom it can serve as a handy checklist.

B.O.C.

v

CONTENTS

CURRICULUM HANDBOOK
FOR
PARENTS AND TEACHERS

Chapter 1

INTRODUCTION

What is a school curriculum? It is what a student is taught in school, a clear statement indicating what skills and information students should acquire in their classes and through their study during any given school year.

Experienced teachers can and do go from one school system to another in this country, receive their class and grade assignments, and know immediately what they will be teaching during the year. The curriculum of the grade is not a mystery to them, so why should it be a mystery to anyone else? It shouldn't be.

Even though fifty state governments in the United States control thousands of independent school systems, education in our country is fairly standard. The curriculum differs little from system to system. It is the way the curriculum is interpreted and used in the classroom where the differences are found.

The particular texts and materials selected for use, the available facilities, the talent and experience of the staff and the preparation, study habits and ability of the students are what distinguishes one school system from another.

This handbook, for parents and other persons who are interested in the public schools, is intended as a quick reference guide. It presents what is usually taught in the schools and the sequence in which it is presented. What is learned depends on the individual student, the school, the home and many other factors.

This is not intended to address regulations nor focus on special programs such as vocational, gifted, religious, handicapped, athletics, or guidance. It focuses on general schools and general offerings.

The content of this handbook was obtained from classroom teachers over a period of years. They were asked to state in concrete terms what they were actually teaching, and the material was collected, reviewed, revised, edited and formatted into a consistent design. How the subject matter is taught, known to educators as "methodology," is not addressed. The focus is on "what" rather than on "how."

USING THIS HANDBOOK

This handbook has two parts:

1. The first part is divided into grades and covers the kindergarten through grade 6. Within every grade section you will find a brief description of the content of each academic area appropriate for that grade.
2. The second part is divided into academic subject areas and is further divided into two parts:
   - A kindergarten through grade 12 overview of the academic area;
   - An expanded grade-by-grade description of the subject matter appropriate for the grade in that particular academic area.

In the Glossary, specialized educational words used throughout this book are defined.

Reading, writing, spelling, speaking and listening skills can be found in Chapter 9, "Language Arts In The Classroom."

It is important to stress that there is a difference between teaching and learning. Before new work for any class or grade can be presented, a level of student readiness is necessary. This readiness level is stated in the expanded curriculum section before the grade's work is described.

Parents, and educators as well, must realize that the primary job of the teacher isn't to "cover" subject matter. It is patently impossible, even given the thirteen years the schools have the students, to "cover," or even just to present, all of the available knowledge in any single field. Certainly, then, an effort to cover all the subject matter in all the academic fields would be impossible.

The true job of the teacher is to "uncover" rather than cover, to give students the tools and insights to understand and to teach them where to find and how to use information. It is also to instill in students the confidence to seek, to imagine, to appreciate, to create and to interact responsibly in society.

ACADEMIC OBJECTIVES—ALL GRADES

GENERAL: To educate every child so that he or she will perform to the best of his or her ability; to recognize and adapt teaching to differences in learning styles of individual students; to teach the basic skills of each academic area.

ART: To foster creativity and inspiration, identify and encourage talent, and provide opportunity for expressing ideas.

BUSINESS: To provide for hands-on use of modern technological instruments, for learning how the economy functions, and for developing skill in business practices.

FOREIGN LANGUAGE: To assist students to achieve vocabulary, grammar, and pronunciation skills which will enable them to participate in conversations, appreciate the culture, read with understanding and translate with facility.

HEALTH EDUCATION: To provide students with basic information concerning nutrition, bodily care, substance abuse, family and sex education and communicable disease.

HOME ECONOMICS: To give students the opportunity to learn basic cooking, sewing and domestic management skills.

INDUSTRIAL ARTS: To give students the opportunity to handle and use basic shop tools in construction and repair.

LANGUAGE ARTS: To help students develop skill in reading, writing, listening and speaking; to foster appreciation for literature and encourage the expression of ideas.

MATHEMATICS: To help students develop facility in managing mathematical processes; to foster appreciation for the function of math in everyday life.

MUSIC: To provide opportunities to sing, play an instrument, read notation, create and enjoy listening to music.

PHYSICAL EDUCATION: To help students learn the elements of sports and games, the value of exercise, basics of lifelong leisure-time activities and sportsmanship.

SCIENCE: To teach students to understand, respect and employ the scientific method in investigating how things work in the world around us; to teach appreciation for the ecology.

SOCIAL STUDIES: To instill knowledge of and respect for the similarities and differences which exist in cultures of people around the world; to provide knowledge of the history and development of humans; to encourage a love of country, good citizenship and good interpersonal relationships.

PART I
CURRICULUM—ELEMENTARY GRADES

Chapter 2

CURRICULUM IN THE ELEMENTARY GRADES

KINDERGARTEN

The kindergarten curriculum contains creative and instructional play, along with formal instruction in many areas. Briefly stated below is the essence of the content in each academic area.

Art

Students are helped to:

- Control use of scissors, crayons, large needles and thread, large paint brushes, clay and clay tools, marking implements, paints, finger paints and plastic materials;
- Recognize and name colors and tools;
- Follow instructions.

Health Education

Instruction is provided in:

- Taking care of the body; parts of the body; five senses; good eating and sleeping habits; street safety; germs and cleanliness;
- Differences between foods and non-food substances; drugs and medicines;
- Family relationships; manners.

Language Arts

Students are instructed in:

READING: Recognizing letters; left to right eye and hand movement; putting pictures in order of occurrence; decoding; memorizing; handling books;

WRITING: Tracing and forming letters; dictating stories; using a computer keyboard; crayoning;

LISTENING: Following verbal directions; telling the difference between sounds; understanding stories; getting along with other children;

9

SPEAKING: Telling things to peers and adults; increasing vocabulary; expressing ideas; recalling details; analyzing.

Mathematics

Instructional focus is on:

- Understanding number concepts through ten;
- Recognizing numerals through ten; copying numerals;
- Understanding concepts of taller, shorter, longer, larger, smaller;
- Recognizing shapes and matching them to their names;
- Counting through twenty; naming and valuing coins; referring to calendars and watches;
- Computer use for simple tasks.

Music

Students learn to:

- Play rhythm instruments; identify sounds of different instruments; recognize note values; identify pitch differences; develop listening skills;
- Participate in singing, dancing and marching; listen to records and sing along.

Physical Education

Students are taught and practice:

- Gross motor skills; floor exercises using the whole body; simple climbing skills; exercises for cardiovascular strength; tumbling and mat skills;
- Basic ball skills; coordination drills; games.

Science

Students are taught:

- The names of the body's senses; how senses are used;
- How to observe and describe objects and changes;
- Properties of water and how it works for us;
- Differences between living and non-living objects;
- Care of plants and animals;
- How to conduct simple experiments.

Social Studies

Students are taught:

- To recognize land and water masses on maps and globes;
- To listen and speak in discussions with classmates;
- To name and identify celebrations appropriate to significant holidays; to sing holiday songs;
- To develop good manners; to understand rules.
- To recognize community helpers; to know their own names and addresses and telephone numbers.

GRADE 1

Art

Opportunities are provided for students to:

- Refine small muscle control when using tools;
- Name colors, textures, tools and processes;
- Use appropriate objects for simple sculpture, stringing beads, sewing, weaving, painting;
- Practice controlled cutting and pasting.

Health Education

Instruction is provided in:

- Good citizenship; sportsmanship; manners;
- Safety in play, on a bicycle, as a pedestrian;

- Care of teeth, eyes, skin, body; standards of nutrition;
- Elementary first aid; germs, shots and medicine;
- Community health workers; family responsibilities.

Language Arts

Students are instructed in:

READING: Recognizing and naming letters of the alphabet; recognizing and building word families; developing a sight vocabulary; matching; putting letters of the alphabet, words, pictures and parts of stories in correct order; responding appropriately to written directions; reading silently and aloud on a pre-primer, primer and book one level with understanding; comprehension; reading simple storybooks for enjoyment;

WRITING: Forming the letters of the alphabet in manuscript; using letters to make and spell words correctly; making up simple sentences; copying; using a computer keyboard;

LISTENING: Recognizing same and different sounds; using phonics to sound out words; identifying synonyms, antonyms, homonyms; identifying beginning, middle and ending sounds; using rhyming words; understanding and following directions;

SPEAKING: Asking and answering questions; conversing; memorizing and reciting; summarizing, telling and retelling stories.

Mathematics

Instructional focus is on:

- Recognizing, writing and putting numbers in correct order up to number 50;
- Addition and subtraction process; immediate response on number facts of single-digit numbers; solving addition and subtraction problems;
- Recognizing and naming shapes; comparing sizes; metric measurement; telling time in half hours;
- Counting by ones, twos, fives and tens; the value of coins; the concept of half; reading a digital clock; using calendar;
- Using a computer and a calculator.

Music

Students are taught to:

- Identify tempo and duration; match tones in singing;
- Identify sounds of rhythm instruments; respond to music with mood, feeling and body movement;
- Develop primary listening skills; identify keyboard notes.
- Sing the national anthem.

Physical Education

Students are taught and practice:

- Safety; listening skills; left-right discrimination;
- Balancing; climbing; hurdling; tunneling; falling;
- Fitness skills; coordination exercises; gross motor skills;
- Ball skills; team games; long and short jump rope skills;
- Moving to music and dancing.

Science

Students are taught:

- Distinguishing characteristics of living and non-living things;
- Methods of investigating the environment; the effects of air and water on the environment;
- How all people are alike and how everyone differs from everyone else; factors necessary for good health;
- The properties and vocabulary of time;
- How to conduct and report on simple experiments.

Social Studies

Students are taught to:

- Construct and use simple maps; recognize locations on globes;
- Appreciate human and other animal family relationships; understand differences in family practices from one culture to another;
- Understand the roles of local community helpers and the importance of local community resources;
- Understand the concepts of seasons, months, holidays;
- Read and remember simple stories related to American history;
- Memorize the words and understand the meaning of the pledge of allegiance.

GRADE 2

Art

Students are taught to:

- Shape, form and assemble using clay, wood, wire, beads and other objects; weave;
- Use inks and stencils for printing;
- Understand balance, rhythm, movement, color use;
- Observe and reproduce detail;
- Understand and follow directions.

Health Education

Instruction is provided in:

- Handling illness; function of hospitals; drugs and medicine;
- Traffic safety; hazards in the environment;
- Cleanliness; body care; nutrition; five main senses and care of the sense organs; the backbone and its function;
- Feelings and managing them; basic emotions;
- Reproduction in lower life forms.

Language Arts

Students are instructed in:

READING: Decoding; increasing sight vocabulary; phonics; using the dictionary; reading with understanding book two in the reading series; introduction to literature; developing skill in sequencing; defining and analyzing words; using grammar correctly; synonyms, antonyms, homonyms; using the library;

WRITING: Creative writing of sentences and paragraphs; spelling; writing from dictation; letter writing; editing; capitalization and punctuation; correct formation and spacing of letters in manuscript; using a computer keyboard;

LISTENING: Responding appropriately to oral directions; analyzing and critiquing oral reports and stories;

SPEAKING: Memorizing and reciting; conversing; making a point; making an oral report; speaking in sentences.

Mathematics

Instructional focus is on:

- Writing, ordering and comparing numbers to 999;
- Adding and subtracting two-digit numbers with and without carrying (regrouping); immediate response on number facts of addition and subtraction; solving number and word problems;
- Dealing with time in minutes, hours, days, weeks, months, years, centuries; using standard and metric measures;
- Understanding symmetry of shapes; using bar, picture and line graphs; reading maps; estimating to ten; making change;
- Using a number line; balancing equations; recognizing inequalities; using a computer and a calculator.

Music

Students learn to:

- Accompany songs with rhythm instruments; sing rounds; use basic music symbols; read simple melodies using numbers and then notes; practice rhythm skills;
- Listen with purpose to music records and recitals.
- Sing a variety of patriotic and other songs.

Physical Education

Students are taught and practice:

- Proper use of indoor and outdoor equipment; safety;
- Awareness of body capability and image; left-right discrimination; gross motor skills; ball skills; balance and climbing skills; coordination exercises; mat and fitness skills; long and short jump rope skills; moving to music.
- Team games; sportsmanship.

Science

Students are taught:

- Properties and vocabulary of sound, including tone, waves, sonar, loudness, softness;
- Qualities of light and shadow, force and friction;
- Causes and effects of weather;
- Life cycles of animals and plants; their interdependence; differ-

ences among animals including how and where they live and what they need to survive;

- Essential steps in conducting and recording experiments.

Social Studies

Students are taught:

- How to recognize symbols for landforms and water bodies on maps and globes; to find and identify the United States;
- To understand and sing the national anthem;
- To appreciate three basic human needs of food, clothing and shelter and their relation to human survival; to discover how humans in the varied environments they encounter on earth provide for these basic needs;
- To understand impact of transportation and communication on various cultures;
- To do simple fact-finding research and write brief reports;
- To understand the qualities of citizenship, leadership, independence and interdependence.

GRADE 3

Art

Instructional focus is placed on:

- Understanding primary, secondary and complementary colors;
- Understanding and using volume, shape, density, weight, height, distance; creating useful objects;
- Composing a work to express emotion and action;
- Cutting linoleum block designs; creating designs;
- Understanding and following directions.

Health Education

Instruction is provided in:

- Caring for & protecting the body, including permanent teeth, posture, feet, sense organs; nutrition and rest;
- Germs, drugs and medicine; hazards of alcohol, tobacco and other addictive substances; safety;
- Expressing feelings; getting along with others;

- Embryonic development.

Language Arts

Students are instructed in:

READING: Decoding; extending sight vocabulary; phonics; diction- ary skills; glossary; table of contents; book three in reading series; use of library for reference and literature; reading aloud to inform and entertain; reading for information; reading with comprehension.

WRITING: Composing letters, postcards and addressing envelopes; writing to inform; creative writing; reports; spelling, grammar and dictation; introduction to cursive writing; using a computer.

LISTENING: Following directions; taking notes; hearing and responding to oral presentation of content material.

SPEAKING: Conversing; grammatical use of the language when speaking; using sentences; memorizing and reciting; oral reporting; convincing.

Mathematics

Instructional focus is on:

- Adding and subtracting multiple-digit numbers with carrying;
- Using number line; reading, writing, ordering and comparing num- bers to 1,000;
- Understanding multiplication as repeated addition, and division as repeated subtraction; multiplication and division facts with immedi- ate response;
- Understanding fractions and mixed numbers; decimal concepts;
- Calculating time and calendar problems; using metric and standard measures; solving number problems; estimating;
- Reading, interpreting and constructing graphs and maps;
- Solving number problems; estimating; identifying shapes; using money for goods and services; solving equations;
- Using a computer and a calculator.

Music

Students are helped to:

- Develop vocal skills; develop better listening skills;
- Identify notes on scale; recognize timbre of instruments;
- Identify form, contrast and repetition in music;

- Choose whether to play an instrument; select instrument;
- Listen to music for enjoyment; move to music.

Physical Education

Help students become more skillful in:

- Ball skills and ball games; relay races;
- Intermediate coordination exercises; mat exercises; balance exercises; aerobic and fitness exercises;
- Proper use of equipment; moving to music and dancing.

Science

Students are taught:

- The properties of rocks and soil; what is learned from soil layers; the effects of heating and cooling on matter;
- How and why thermometers are used; centigrade and Fahrenheit;
- Features and interactions of the sun, earth, moon, planets, stars, constellations; space travel; observation skills;
- Static and circuit electricity; objects which are conductors or insulators; safety rules for using electricity;
- Adaptation and behavior of animals and plants in their environments; interdependence of plants, animals, humans.

Social Studies

Students are taught:

- Map skills; use of legends, scales, interpretating color, hemispheres; locating home state, county, city, town;
- Locating and using information found in a dictionary, atlas, glossary, almanac, encyclopedia;
- The geography, history and economic development of specific communities; contributions of native Americans and immigrant groups to the culture of America; interdependence of persons and communities; student's neighborhood as a community; the community as part of a country;
- Rights and responsibilities of a citizen in a community.

GRADE 4

Art

Instructional focus is placed on:

- Understanding elements of art design; art appreciation;
- Using materials imaginatively; reproducing natural forms;
- Controlling use of clay paint, scissors, cutting tools, paste, paper, wood, wire, plaster, threads and string.

Health Education

Instruction is provided in:

- Caring for the body; nutrition; first aid for cuts and burns; understanding the body's protective mechanisms; growth timetables; how bones mend; how cuts heal;
- Safety; germs, drugs and medicine; use and abuse of hazardous and addictive substances;
- Male and female anatomical attributes.

Language Arts

Instructional focus is on:

READING: Decoding, defining and analyzing new words; comprehending; identifying main idea; finding details; critically evaluating; book four in reader; increasing sight vocabulary; study skills; fluent reading aloud; use of reference books in library and classroom; reading for content; reading literature for appreciation;

WRITING: Creative and factual composition; reports; spelling rules; rules of grammar, punctuation, capitalization; improved control of cursive writing; outlining; writing from dictation; use of computer;

LISTENING: Critical listening; taking notes; listening for content and remembering; following oral directions;

SPEAKING: Conversing; presenting ideas and information fluently; using standard pronunciation; memorizing and reciting poems and prose; convincing.

Mathematics

Instructional focus is on:

- Adding, subtracting, multiplying and dividing multiple-digit numbers with carrying; solving word and number problems;

- Reading, writing and comparing numbers up to millions;
- Place value; immediate response on number facts;
- Rounding numbers to nearest tenth, hundreth, thousandth;
- Metric measurements; perimeter, shapes, angles, length;
- Fractions; decimals; time and calendar problems;
- Tables, graphs, maps, charts; estimating;
- Money concepts to nearest dollar and ten dollars;
- Roman numerals; number and numeral; equations;
- Using a computer and a calculator.

Music

Students refine ability to:

- Identify pitch and rhythm patterns; recognize major scales and tone colors; sing two-part songs; sing in chorus;
- Play instruments and read music; read notes on a musical staff and recognize note value;
- Enhance listening skills and music appreciation.

Physical Education

Students are helped to:

- Improve rhythmic and motor skills and coordination;
- Participate in isometric and isotonic conditioning; controlled breathing; dynamic and static balance; tumbling;
- Play competitively through: jump roping; ball games; group and team sports; dance; moving rhythmically to music;
- Proper use and care of equipment.

Science

Instructional focus is on:

- History of the earth's changing surface; using maps, globes and charts to obtain and share information;
- Properties and vocabulary of light including reflection, refraction, lenses, lasers, waves; forces causing change;
- Weather and atmospheric conditions; use of measuring instruments for weather; how to record data; forecasting;
- Populations and communities (animal & human);
- Properties and vocabulary of simple and compound machines, including: force, direction, distance, speed, power;

- Food chains, networks and webs; human impact on environment;
- Classification of plants and animals;
- Observation and data collection in experiments.

Social Studies

Instructional focus is on:

- Use of maps to identify ocean currents, sea levels, weather, political subdivisions, elevations, variety in typical regions of the earth regarding landforms, climate, culture, government, natural resources, occupations and their interdependence; economic geography; impact on human culture of living in forests, deserts, plains, mountains and near or in oceans (on islands);
- History and geography of home state and contiguous states;
- Use of encyclopedia, almanac and appendices for research; note taking; outlining; crediting sources on written reports; interviewing techniques;
- Discovery and exploration of America;
- Rights and responsibilities of citizens in communities.

GRADE 5

Art

Instructional focus is on:

- Examining forms and variations, symbols, illusions;
- Understanding and using color interactions;
- Drawing, painting and modeling people, animals and objects; weaving; using various media; art appreciation; artists.

Health Education

Instruction is provided in:

- Caring for the body; nutrition; effect of substance abuse;
- Function and protection of the brain; blood types; function of blood in the body; visual and auditory defects; diseases and medicines; germs, drugs and medication;
- Emotional development; male and female body changes in adolescence; menstruation.

Language Arts

Instructional focus is on:

READING: Decoding and vocabulary development; interpreting characterization; recognizing differences between fact and opinion; skillful use of reference materials; extracting information; book five in reader; reading literature for comprehension, enjoyment and appreciation; using library; reading aloud to inform and entertain;

WRITING: Applying grammatical and spelling rules to creative and expository writing; using proper paragraphing, word-order punctuation, capitalization; outlining, taking notes and writing reports; cursive writing practice; using a computer and typewriter;

LISTENING: Aurally obtaining content from oral presentation; conversing; convincing; distinguishing standard speech patterns from regionalisms; following directions;

SPEAKING: Memorizing and reciting; pronunciation; expanded vocabulary; presenting an argument; relaying a message.

Mathematics

Instructional focus is on:

- Using the four basic operations $(+, -, \times, \div)$ on multiple-digit numbers; immediate response on number facts; estimating and rounding; solving problems; identity elements (0 and 1); least common multiple; greatest common factor; finding averages; operations on fractions and decimals;
- Horizontal, vertical; diameter and circumference;
- Roman numerals; ordinal numbers; negative numbers;
- Graphs, graphics, maps, tables; equations; inequalities;
- Standard and metric measures including temperature;
- Using a calculator and a computer.

Music

Instructional focus is on:

- Identification of syncopation and various dance rhythms; homophony and polyphony; reading music on a staff;
- Music of ballet, opera, concerto, symphony;
- Two-part singing; singing for fun; moving to music;

- Performing in orchestra or band or chorus.

Physical Education

Instructional focus is on:

- Rules for a variety of games; practicing interaction skills; cooperation and independence; sportsmanship;
- Honing skills used in: gymnastics and tumbling, balance and coordination; aerobics; dance and moving rhythmically to music; ball and rope activities;
- Proper use and care of equipment.

Science

Instructional focus is on:

- Characteristics and importance of the oceans, waves, tides, currents, ocean floors and ocean life forms;
- Structure and function of the sense organs of the human body; the human digestive, circulatory, respiratory and excretory systems; a balanced diet; harmful effects of tobacco, alcohol and addictive drugs on the body systems;
- Constellations and gallaxies; solar system;
- Series and parallel circuits; magnetic fields of force and electric current;
- Specific characteristics of the scientific method and its reliance on experimentation and observation.

Social Studies

Instructional focus is on:

- Use of maps to trace the journeys of early explorers of America; to understand and use concepts of longitude and latitude, time zones, the equator, the polar regions, the Tropic of Cancer and the Tropic of Capricorn;
- Overview of history of the United States; concepts of democratic government; appreciation of contributions of great men and women to the history of the country;
- Likenesses and differences of major sections of the country in geography, history and culture;
- Names, capitals, major cities and major natural resources of each of the United States;

- Names and locations of countries of the world;
- Refining and improving research and study skills.

GRADE 6

Art

Instructional focus is on:

- Studying elements of art history; art appreciation;
- Using basic principles of perspective with line and color to create illusion of third dimension;
- Working in available media; using appropriate processes;
- Refining taste and technique.

Health Education

Instruction focus is on:

- Grooming; handling emotions in stressful situations;
- Disease and community responsibility; effects of substance abuse; poisons; nutrition; safety;
- Renowned scientists' contributions to health;
- Ecology and pollution;
- Male and female development; human fertilization.

Language Arts

Instructional focus is on:

READING: Increasing comprehension and appreciation; using the library; expansion of vocabulary; figures of speech, imagery, idioms; improving reading speed; fluent oral reading; book six in reader; reading for information; reading literature;

WRITING: Control of cursive writing skills; creating short stories, poetry, reports; spelling and grammar rules; taking notes and making outlines; capitalization, punctuation, paragraphing; using a computer;

LISTENING: Taking notes on content from oral presentations; following directions; conversing; convincing.

SPEAKING: Presenting information concisely; memorizing and reciting; expanded vocabulary; accurate reporting.

Mathematics

Instructional focus is on:

- Using four basic operations on multiple-digit numbers, fractions, decimals; problems; consumer math;
- Using standard and metric measures for temperature and liquids; volume;
- Mean; median; properties of triangles, rectangles, squares; equations; ratio and proportion; percent;
- Estimating and rounding; writing numbers up to twelve digits; problem solving; Roman numerals; ordinals, negative numbers; tables, graphs, maps, charts;
- Using a calculator and a computer.

Music

Instructional focus is on:

- Discriminating between sounds of major and minor scales;
- Singing major and harmonic minor scales from written music with and without accompaniment; singing for fun;
- Listening to music for appreciation; moving to music;
- Performing in orchestra, band or chorus.

Physical Education

Instructional focus is on:

- Review of game and sports skills taught;
- Advanced coordination activities; more difficult balance, gymnastic and mat skills; aerobics; dancing and moving rhythmically to music;
- Ball and rope activities; relays and individual races;
- Proper use and care of equipment.

Science

Instructional focus is on:

- Newton's laws of motion; the effects of gravity and other forces on mass; structure and conservation of matter;
- Classification of substances and of living things; fossils and what they have taught us about gelogical change; plant, animal, and protist microorganisms;
- Conservation of energy; natural resources and ecology;

- Reproduction and heridity in living things; learning and reasoning processes in lower animals and in humans;
- Observation and data collection as essentials in the scientific method.

Social Studies

Instructional focus is on:

- Tracing routes of the explorers of Latin America and Canada;
- Discovery of reversal of seasons and change in air and water circulation patterns in the Southern Hemisphere;
- Equatorial and polar temperatures and their cultural impact;
- History, geography and variety of cultures to be found in Latin America and Canada; locating and identifying the geographical features, resources and economic development of the major areas of Latin America and Canada;
- Colonialism, regionalism, revolution and politics in Canada and Latin America; comparing and contrasting these with similar happenings in American history;
- Practice and review of basic study skills including note taking; focus on current events and citizenship.

PART II
CURRICULUM CONTENT—
SUBJECT BY SUBJECT

Chapter 3

ART IN THE CLASSROOM

OVERVIEW

Art is taught as an integral part of the subject matter of all the elementary grades. Some school systems also have an art requirement in grades 7, 8 and 9. Beyond that, art is usually offered as an elective.

Grade K—Opportunities are provided for students to: control use of scissors, crayons, large needles and thread, large paint brushes, clay and clay tools, marking implements, paints, finger paints, plastic materials; recognize and name colors and tools; follow instructions.

Grade 1—Opportunities are provided for students to: refine small muscle control using tools; name colors, textures, tools, processes; use appropriate objects for simple sculpture, sewing, stringing beads, weaving; practice controlled cutting and pasting.

Grade 2—Instructional focus is placed on: shaping, forming and assembling using clay, wood, wire, beads and other objects; using inks and stencils for printing; weaving; understanding use of balance, rhythm, color; movement; observing and reproducing detail; understanding and following directions.

Grade 3—Instructional focus is placed on: understanding primary, secondary and complementary colors; understanding and using shape, volume, density, weight, height, distance; composing a work to express emotion and action; designing; creating useful objects; linoleum block designs; following directions.

Grade 4—Instructional focus is placed on: understanding elements of art design; using materials imaginatively; appreciating artistic products; controlling use of clay paint, scissors, cutting tools, paste, paper, wood, wire, plaster, threads and string; seeing and reproducing natural forms.

Grade 5—Instructional focus is placed on: examining forms and variations, symbols, illusions; developing discernment and taste; understanding and using color interactions; drawing, painting, and modeling people, animals and objects; weaving; art appreciation.

Grade 6—Instructional focus is placed on: studying elements of art history; using basic principles of perspective with line and color to create illusion of third dimension; working with all available materials; using all appropriate processes; art appreciation; refining taste and techniques.

The following are typical of art courses offered in secondary schools. Most students elect to take some art.

Grade 7—Instructional focus is on: using perspective to establish space; line drawing from real objects; creating with tempra, paper mache, water color, plastic materials; block prints; lives and works of famous artists; expanding art vocabulary.

Grade 8—Instructional focus is placed on: drawing figure contours; constructing collages; batik; lettering design; relief painting printing; constructing ceramics; solving three-dimensional problems; extending research into art history.

DRAWING, PAINTING, SCULPTURE (In combination or separately). *Students are provided with opportunities to:* use a range of media and techniques to draw, paint, sculpt; study the human figure, plants and animals, in terms of design and function; use acrylic, water color, oils, pencil, pen and ink, silver point, clay and plaster; use and care for tools appropriate to medium.

PHOTOGRAPHY AND ADVANCED PHOTOGRAPHY (In schools where there are darkroom facilities available). *Students are taught to:* use the camera to produce art; develop various photographic techniques; set up and use a darkroom; use filters; mount and frame photographs; create a portfolio; critique.

ART MAJOR I, II, III (For students who wish to take Art every year). *Focus is concentrated on:* finding creative solutions to problems in graphics and aesthetics and use of media; critiquing; using all available media and tools; examining careers in art; learning history of and appreciating works of great artists; studio performance and preparation of one-person shows.

Besides these basics, some schools offer additional courses which may include the following as well as others:

- History of film and filmmaking
- Wood and stone carving

- Weaving and textiles
- Jewelry making
- Pottery and ceramics
- Art History and Appreciation

ART IN THE CLASSROOM

Grade K

Coming into the class a student should demonstrate ability to:

- Listen and follow directions;
- Hold and use brushes and crayons;
- Recognize similarities and differences;
- Show emotions when telling about something;
- Enjoy working independently.

In the grade students are taught to:

- Recognize, name and match colors;
- Use appropriate tools for each project including crayons, paints, large paint brushes, finger paints, pencils;
- Cut, paste, tear and construct;
- Construct with clay, wood, wire, cardboard and found objects; use large needles and thread;
- Name forms; judge sizes and positions;
- Care for, clean and store tools.

Grade 1

Coming into the grade a student should be able to:

- Recognize and name colors; use paint and large brushes, clay and clay tools; scissors;
- Follow instructions.

In the grade students are taught to:

- Achieve greater control of small muscle activities;
- Use scissors for controlled cutting;
- Paste objects in appropriate spaces;
- Name tools in use and art or craft objects produced;
- Construct three-dimensional objects using clay, wood, wire, paper, found objects;
- String beads, sew with large needles; do simple weaving;
- Talk about pictures and what is depicted in them;
- Name, use, and combine colors;
- Identify shapes, sizes, relative positions;
- Follow simple written directions;
- Clean, care for and store tools appropriately.

Grade 2

Coming into the grade a student should be able to:

- Identify colors, shapes sizes, relative positions;
- Work with clay, paints, crayons, finger paints, pencils;
- Follow simple written and oral instructions;
- Work independently; demonstrate interest in producing art.

In the grade students are taught to:

- Select, arrange and discuss objects used in producing art;
- Shape, form and assemble three-dimensional products using clay, wood, wire, beads, threads, cord and found objects;
- Use inks and stencils to produce art;
- Examine and describe pictures concentrating on colors and visible details; observe and reproduce details;
- Draw and paint pictures and tell about them;
- Stitch and weave; cut and paste with control;
- Understand concepts of balance, rhythm and movement in art;
- Recognize and discuss volume and variety of shapes;

- Appreciate artwork produced by others;
- Clean, care for and store tools appropriately.

Grade 3

Coming into the grade a student should be able to:

- Follow written and oral instructions;
- Manipulate and control the use of basic tools of art;
- Concentrate, and complete projects;
- Work willingly, with interest and confidence;
- Show understanding of basic art concepts of balance, rhythm, movement, size, relative positions.

In the grade students are taught to:

- Draw and paint pictures with conscious control of colors, shapes, sizes and placement of objects; cut and paste;
- Name and use primary, secondary and complementary colors;
- Create three-dimensional projects using a variety of media;
- Use linoleum blocks, carved vegetables, found objects, to make prints; use a variety of carving tools safely;
- Design a paper using basic art principles of color, balance, form, rhythm, movement, shape, volume and size;
- Use art to express emotion, action; depict the environment;
- Use critical judgment and discrimination;
- Clean, care for and store tools appropriately.

Grade 4

Coming into the grade a student should be able to:

- Represent real things in two and three dimensions using a variety of media; discuss artwork produced;
- Demonstrate understanding of primary, complementary and secondary colors and their use for effect; mix colors;
- Use art tools safely and effectively.

In the grade students are taught to:

- Use elements of art design including repetition, variety, patterns, contrast, composition;
- Examine great art and recognize what makes it great;
- Critically self-evaluate products; value originality;
- Use materials, media, and tools imaginatively;

- Achieve greater control when working with clay, paint, scissors, crayons, pencils, paste, paper, plaster, wood, wire, thread;
- Observe natural forms and reproduce them; illustrate;
- Participate in classroom projects and discussions about art;
- Critique with understanding of basic principles and taste;
- Clean, care for and store tools appropriately.

Grade 5

Coming into the grade a student should be able to:

- Recognize some famous works of art;
- Critique classroom art with some understanding and taste;
- Demonstrate control of media and tools;
- Demonstrate understanding of composition and design;
- Demonstrate knowledge of color principles;
- Demonstrate ability to observe and reproduce form.

In the grade students are taught to:

- Work with forms and variations to create design;
- Interpret and use symbols to represent concepts and objects;
- Use line and color combinations to create mood, illusion;
- Observe humans and other animals and use them as models for creating two- and three-dimensional art; weave and knot to make textiles; design with needles and thread;
- Examine and appreciate works of art; research famous artists;
- Clean, care for and store tools appropriately.

Grade 6

Coming into the grade a student should be able to:

- Discuss the works and lives of some of the great artists;
- Depict human and animal forms in two and three dimensions;
- Use elements of design in creating art compositions;
- Use varieties of materials and tools to best advantage;
- Demonstrate taste and ability to critique.

In the grade students are taught to:

- Appreciate and understand elements of art history and works of famous artists;
- Use perspective and shading to create an illusion of three dimensions on a two-dimensional surface;

- Use materials and tools with discrimination and control;
- Create art considering color, form, balance and design;
- Develop brush control in painting to create effects;
- Combine materials to produce original artwork;
- Build ceramics using coil and slab; create relief prints;
- Weave, incorporating designs; create macrame products;
- Use papier-mache, cut, paste and carve to create sculpture;
- Work with peers on a large effort like a mural;
- Clean, care for and store tools appropriately.

Grade 7

Coming into the grade a student should be able to:

- Create three-dimensional art by modeling, carving and constructing; use tools appropriately;
- Understand and use principles of perspective;
- Mix and use colors in painting; select brushes to create effects; use simple printing techniques;
- Create woven materials, knotted materials and stitched work.

In the grade students are taught to:

- Establish space on planes; use vanishing points;
- Do contour and line drawings from actual objects;
- Combine factual drawing with creative invention and design;
- Mix colors to achieve shades and tints;
- Use water inks and brayers to print from raised surfaces;
- Construct objects using papier-mache;
- Research and report on aspects of art history; view slides;
- Understand the variety of careers open to artists;
- Combine line, color and form to create mood;
- Combine shapes for interest, unity, balance, contrast.

Grade 8

Coming into the grade a student should be able to:

- Discuss the elements of design;
- Paint using primary and secondary colors, and mixtures;
- Print reliefs and print from raised surfaces;
- Sculpt using modeling and carving techniques;
- Use form, color, line and space to create effects.

In the grade students are taught to:

- Do creative contour drawing; use pastels:
- Create collages using variety of materials and techniques;
- Use letters of the alphabet to create designs, patterns;
- Use positive and negative space and shapes in design;
- Use texture and color to create effects; design with batik;
- Treat surfaces with glazes, fixatifs and patinas;
- Carve relief designs and combine form with surface interest;
- Recognize names and works of famous artists;
- Select appropriate materials and tools for creative work;
- Appreciate modern trends in art and design;
- Clean, care for and store tools appropriately.

Grades 9–12: *Drawing, Painting, Sculpture*

(Some schools offer these options as one class. Others offer them separately. The curriculum described below is as a single course.)

Coming into the class a student should demonstrate ability to:

- Draw, paint, sculpt, from a model or still life;
- Work with color using brushes, paints, pencil, charcoal, pastels; use sculptural materials and tools;
- Discuss the lives and works of some famous artists.

In the grade students are taught to:

- Produce designed art using still-life constructions and live models as subjects;
- See and reproduce line, gesture and form;
- Understand the importance of inner structure in producing artistic surfaces; construct a supporting armature for sculpture; construct, stretch and prime a canvas;
- Use color as an expressive component in art;
- Use a variety of painting materials and techniques including acrylics, oils, water colors;
- Use a variety of materials including clay, wood, plaster, paper, plastics and metal for sculpture;
- Use various surface finishes in three-dimensional work;
- Use pencils, pens, inks, silverpoint, charcoal and pastels for drawing;
- Appreciate the use of art as a means of communication;
- Appreciate works of great artists of the past and present;

- Make maximum use of individual creativity and inventiveness;
- Develop awareness of placement and scale in making visual statements; critique and discuss works created in class;
- Create pottery on a wheel;
- Create spatial designs involving shape relationships;
- Understand the range of careers open to artists;
- Clean, care for and store tools appropriately.

Grades 10–12: Photography and Advanced Photography

(These courses may or may not be offered, depending on the teacher talent and the equipment available in a school.)

Coming into the class a student should demonstrate ability to:

- Operate a camera;
- Read and follow directions.

In the class students are taught to:

- Understand limitations and abilities of particular cameras;
- Understand lenses and their capabilities;
- Understand the interdependence of film, light and lenses;
- Understand the use of a light meter and filters;
- Process an exposed roll of film including mixing chemicals and step-by-step developing to produce printable negatives;
- Produce an artistic, expressive print; use a darkroom;
- Recognize the elements of good versus poor composition;
- Research into photography of the past and present;
- Dodge, crop and enlarge; compose a photograph;
- Critique appropriately; use photography to produce art;
- Clean, care for and store materials appropriately.

Grades 10–12: Art Major

(These courses are offered to students who elect to major in art. Students may take one, two, or all three years of study.)

Coming into the class a student should demonstrate ability to:

- Work creatively and independently using a full range of materials and tools;
- Work with concentration and carry a work through to its completion; critique works of art;
- Use art and design principles effectively and aesthetically.

In these classes students are taught to:

- Draw accurately and with distortion used for effect;
- Use shading, colors, texture for creating the illusion of solids;
- Use dry point etching, collage; silk screen for reproduction; draw with ebony pencils;
- Use solvents in adhering and dissolving processes;
- Use nitric acid on zinc for etching; intaglio;
- Create patterns for textile design;
- Prepare work for presentation including matting, framing, using pedestals and easels;
- Produce portraits in paint and clay, additive techniques in sculpture; use wheel, kiln and glazes in making pottery;
- Understand and appreciate history of art, great artists, styles of art; investigate careers in art;
- Develop and maintain a portfolio; mount a "one-man show."

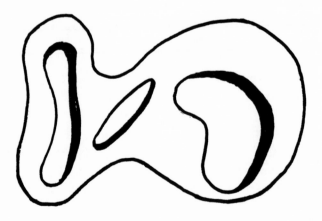

Chapter 4

BUSINESS IN THE CLASSROOM

OVERVIEW

Courses are offered in this area to assist students who want to develop personal skills, or to prepare for entry-level business jobs and/or for business courses in college-level study. Not every school system offers the same selection, and all the offerings described are secondary school electives.

KEYBOARDING AND PERSONAL TYPING (Generally one semester). *Instructional focus is on:* providing opportunity to practice quick and accurate touch typing for students who want to develop facility in working with typewriters and computer keyboards; formatting and mechanics of page design for term papers, business and personal letters.

KEYBOARDING AND ADVANCED TYPING —(Generally one semester) *Instructional focus is on:* practicing correct typing skills to achieve at least 35 words per minute; accuracy in proofreading, spelling, grammar and punctuation.

SHORTHAND I AND II: Students focus on: using symbols and principles of a chosen shorthand system; construction of phrases; speed-building techniques; taking dictation at the rate of 60 words per minute; transcribing shorthand notes into accurate typewritten documents; proofreading techniques.

MARKETING—DISTRIBUTIVE EDUCATION I AND II: Students focus on: basics of marketing; human relations in marketing; packaging techniques; displaying merchandise; window display; store math; fashions; cash register use; understanding trade reports and journals; buying plans; sales promotion; salesmanship; techniques of advertising; resumes; techniques of job interviewing; grooming; channels of distribution; using the media; using tape recorders, videotapes, video cameras; collecting and paying taxes; keeping records.

ACCOUNTING: Students focus on: analysis of typical business trans-

39

actions; setting up a ledger; using accounts; closing a ledger; electronic data processing; spread sheets; bad debts and depreciation; accruals and deferrals; accounting equations; financial statements; accounting simulations; computerized accounting systems.

ADVANCED ACCOUNTING: Students focus on: proprietorship and partnership accounting; incorporating; analysis of financial statements; control of accounts payable and accounts receivable; accruals; corporation accounting; cost accounting; inventory controls; depreciation; bad debts; accounting cycles; taxes and tax preparation; computerized accounting systems.

WORD PROCESSING: Students focus on: use of electronic typewriters, computer and word processing software; symbols and codes needed to control word processor; making maximum use of software; duplicating techniques; care and maintenance of equipment; appropriate storage and filing techniques.

INTRODUCTION TO THE COMPUTER: Students focus on: learning a computer language (generally "Basic" is learned); system commands; writing programs; debugging; capabilities of a computer; input and output devices; storing devices; memory-expanding devices; modems and bulletin boards; choosing and using software.

BUSINESS ECONOMICS—Students focus on: understanding gross national product (GNP), national income, consumer price index (CPI), national debt; understanding the role of government in the American economy; in economies of other countries; international economic interdependence; the workings of the Federal Reserve System and commercial banks concerning money and credit; understanding the stock market, the bond market and the commodities market; local, state and federal taxation programs; inflation, recession, depression, free enterprise; capitalism, socialism, communism.

As in several other curriculum areas, school systems vary in number and types of courses offered by business departments of secondary schools. In addition to the above, some schools provide instruction in courses including but not limited to:

- Computer languages: Pascal, Cobol, Fortran
- Computer software: Lotus, Wordstar, Smartkey, etc.
- Cooperative Industrial Education (CIE)
- Cooperative Vocational Education (CVE)

BUSINESS IN THE CLASSROOM

Grades 8–12: *Keyboarding and Personal Typing* (Usually one semester)

Coming into the class a student should demonstrate ability to:

- Read and write;
- Follow written directions;
- Work independently with concentration.

In the class students are taught:

- Names and uses of the parts of a typewriter and of a computer keyboard; care of the keyboard and platen;
- Procedures for inserting, straightening and removing paper;
- How to set margins, tabs, center a paper;
- Keyboard fingering, stroking technique, touch typing;
- Methods of error correction; proofreading techniques;
- How to touch type at the rate of at least 20 words per minute with no more than three errors.
- Formats for business and personal letters; formats for term papers, headings, footnotes, bibliographies.

Grades 9–12: *Keyboarding and Advanced Typing*

Coming into the class a student should demonstrate ability to:

- Touch type at the rate of 20 words a minute or faster;
- Operate a keyboard effectively;
- Work independently with concentration.

In the class students are taught to:

- Type a ruled table; type a form;
- Determine a bottom margin with and without footnotes;
- Design a page for specific purposes, including: book manuscript, news release, term paper, letter;
- Write a formal business letter; type an envelope;
- Proofread accurately; spell correctly;
- Use correct grammar and punctuation;
- Touch-type at the rate of at least 35 words per minute with no more than three errors on a five-minute exercise;
- Care for a typewriter and a computer keyboard.

Grades 10–12: Shorthand I and Shorthand II

Coming into the class a student should demonstrate ability to:

- Read, speak and write with facility;
- Write with correct grammar and spelling skills;
- Listen with concentration.

In the class students are taught:

- The basic symbols of the shorthand system chosen;
- Brief forms and derivatives;
- Methods used for constructing phrases;
- Skills needed to read shorthand;
- Speed-building techniques for shorthand (to 100 W.P.M.) and typing (to 50 W.P.M. when transcribing from shorthand);
- Machine transcription procedures;
- Taking dictation and transcribing from diversified material;
- Business vocabulary; correct spelling, punctuation, grammar;
- Businesslike work habits; use of reference materials.

Grades 11–12: Marketing and Distributive Education I and II

Coming into the class a student should demonstrate ability to:

- Function with ease and accuracy when adding, subtracting, multiplying and dividing;
- Compute fractions, percents, simple interest;
- Convert fractions to decimals and vice versa;
- Speak and write intelligibly.

In the class students are taught to:

- Handle money and sales checks and operate a cash register;
- Set up a display and a window display with materials at hand; make a sales presentation;
- Markup and markdown tickets; complete inventory sheets;
- Design advertisements; tape a radio comercial and a video;

- Design a package; market a product;
- Use a telephone appropriately;
- Handle customer's inquiries and complaints;
- Compute taxes; keep appropriate records;
- Dress appropriately for business;
- Design a resume and apply for a job;
- Merchandise fashions; manage a department; manage a store;
- Buy and price for profit.

Grades 11-12: Accounting

Coming into the class a student should demonstrate ability to:

- Add, subtract, multiply and divide with facility;
- Handle simple and compound interest problems;
- Convert fractions to decimals and vice versa;
- Solve ratio and percent problems.

In the class students are taught to:

- Understand and analyze business transactions;
- Set up accounts; open and close a ledger;
- Compute a trial balance; develop a financial statement;
- Set up a payroll; oversee banking activities;
- Process cash receipts and cash payments;
- Handle accruals and deferrals;
- Process merchandise purchases;
- Use a computer program and set up a spread sheet;
- Use electric and electronic calculators;
- Understand taxes and tax forms.

Grade 12: Advanced Accounting

Coming into the class a student should demonstrate ability to:

- Handle all processes taught in Accounting;
- Keep accurate records.

In the class students are taught to:

- Understand and use business vocabulary appropriately;
- Understand the accounting cycle;
- Handle the financial transactions of a proprietorship, partnership and a corporation;
- Understand and complete personal and business tax forms;

- Set up voucher systems; spread sheets;
- Account for fixed assets; bad debts and depreciation;
- Set up controls on inventories, accounts payable, accounts receivable, purchases and sales; monitor payroll accounts;
- Use computer programs for accounting purposes.

Grades 8-12: Introduction to the Computer

Coming into the class a student should demonstrate ability to:

- Understand and use all basic arithmetic processes;
- Understand and follow directions;
- Use a computer keyboard.

In the class students are taught to:

- Start up and shut down a computer;
- Use appropriate system commands to input data, access files and programs, store data;
- Use the language statements needed to write programs (Basic); write, debug, and use simple programs;
- Select software programs for specific uses;
- Access information on storage devices (tapes, disks);
- Use output devices appropriately;
- Understand use of modems to access bulletin boards;
- Understand the principles of the base 2 system;
- Understand how the ASCI language is used by the computer;
- Understand how a computer works, how to expand memory and the differences among computers.

Grades 10-12: Word Processing

Coming into the class a student should demonstrate ability to:

- Touch type at least 20 words a minute;

- Type letters and manuscripts in proper form;
- Use a typewriter and a computer keyboard effectively.

In the class students are taught to:

- Use an electric typewriter, an electronic typewriter and a computer keyboard interchangeably;
- Understand and use the appropriate codes for selected word processing software;
- Understand and use a printer with form feeds and cut sheets;
- Make corrections on a computer-typed document;
- Produce multiple copies with a computer and with a copier;
- Use software as an assistant in proofreading;
- Understand and practice proper techniques of care for word processing machines.
- Make and keep copies and use software techniques for filing.

Grades 10–12: Business Economics

Coming into the class a student should demonstrate ability to:

- Ability to do arithmetic and some algebra;
- Ability to read with understanding.

In the class students are taught:

- How society produces and distributes goods and services;
- Land, labor and capital management;
- The role of governments in national economies and international interdependence;
- Role of the consumer; free enterprise; supply and demand;
- National income (NI); gross national product (GNP); consumer price index (CPI); national debt; federal reserve commission (the fed);
- Credit; interest rates; commercial banks; mortgages;
- Local, state and federal tax structures; the public debt;
- Types of business organizations;
- Capitalism, socialism, communism;
- Workings of the stock market, bond market, commodities market;
- Economic problems including: unemployment, social programs, inflation, recession, depression.
- Graphing of trends.

Chapter 5

FOREIGN LANGUAGE IN THE CLASSROOM

OVERVIEW

Different foreign languages are offered by each school system. Some offer only one or two languages, some offer more. Some schools begin teaching foreign languages in elementary grades, taking advantage of the ease with which younger children pick up languages. However, most schools start teaching foreign languages in grade seven and concentrate instruction in grades nine through twelve.

Among the popular languages offered are French, Spanish, Italian, Latin, Greek, Russian, Chinese, Japanese, Hebrew.

Some students study two languages in the secondary school. Those who do generally take two years of one and three years of another. Many students concentrate on only one language and take the full offering in that language.

(LANGUAGE I is the first year of any language on any grade level; LANGUAGE II follows, as do the rest, in sequence.)

LANGUAGE I—Instruction includes: introduction to sound and characteristics of the language; training the ear to hear and the voice to create native sounds; presentation of between 500 and 1,000 vocabulary words which students pronounce and use in context; study of grammar and syntax; introduction to some idioms; study of the culture of the people who use the language; appreciation of the influence of the language on English and vice versa; translating to and from English in oral and written form.

LANGUAGE II—Instruction includes: practice in facility with oral and written vocabulary; opportunity to converse; improving accent, intonation and ability with aural discrimination; using correct grammar, syntax and idiomatic expressions; writing original statements; writing from dictation; reading and translating literature written in the language; oral and written translation to and from English.

LANGUAGE III—Instruction includes: reading literature of the lan-

guage in the original and in translation; developing proficiency in conversing with appropriate accent and intonation; increasing proficiency in both listening and speaking; writing from dictation; creative composition; increased understanding of grammar and syntax of language; developing ability to think in the language.

LANGUAGE IV—Students are helped to: achieve proficient oral-aural language command; read extensively in literature of the language with facility in translating; develop extensive command of grammar and vocabulary; increase ability to think in the language; use the language as a tool in pursuit of other goals.

LANGUAGE V—Students are helped to: read literature of the language for content and appreciation; achieve proficiency in conversation and in functional use of the language; develop expertise in using the grammar and vocabulary of the language; write expository compositions and creative material in the language.

FOREIGN LANGUAGE IN THE CLASSROOM

Grades 7-12: Foreign Language I

Coming into the class a student should demonstrate ability to:

- Understand and use appropriate grammar in native language;
- Read, write, speak and spell correctly in native language.

In the class students are taught to:

- Pronounce words; hear and produce the proper intonation;
- Learn to read, translate and speak using between 500 and 1,000 words;
- Carry on simple conversations in the new language;
- Write words, phrases and sentences from dictation;
- Create short written paragraphs;
- Translate short paragraphs;
- Listen to records with understanding; sing simple songs;

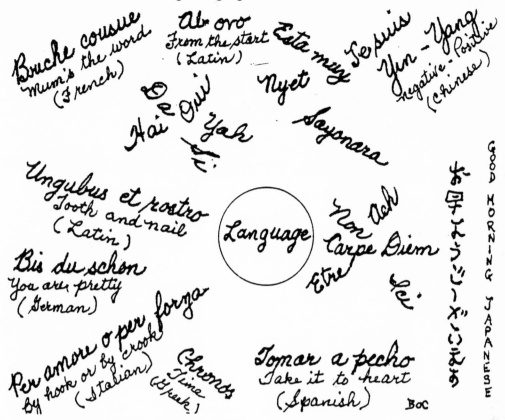

- Use nouns with correct articles; learn gender differences of words if appropriate;
- Use adjectives and place them appropriately vis-à-vis nouns; use adverbs as modifiers correctly positioned in sentences; use prepositions and prepositional phrases; use singular and plural pronouns with correct gender;
- Conjugate regular and irregular verbs; use verbs correctly with reference to time, place, number and complexity;
- Use appropriate idioms;
- Understand and appreciate the culture(s) for which the language is native; memorize and recite some simple poems;
- Recite the alphabet; memorize the numbers; identify days of the week, months of the year; tell time; name colors;
- Keep a notebook.

Grades 8–12: Foreign Language II

Coming into the class a student should demonstrate ability to:

- Read, pronounce and translate vocabulary words correctly;
- Participate in simple conversations in the language;
- Understand and use proper verb forms;
- Translate passages from books.

In the class students are taught to:

- Expand sight vocabulary and begin to develop skill in defining words in the language rather than in translation;
- Conjugate verbs and use proper verb forms to express present, past, future, conditional, etc.;
- Use pronouns and place them correctly in sentences;
- Expand the use of idiomatic expressions;
- Use adjectives and adverbs to modify nouns and verbs;
- Write with accuracy all of the words in the spoken vocabulary; write accurately from dictation;
- Converse understandably without constant reference to English; listen and speak (aural-oral);
- Read and translate into English, passages from literature of the language; translate English passages into the language;
- Understand and appreciate the current events of the countries using the language;
- Use proper accent and intonation when speaking the language;
- Memorize several songs and poems in the language;
- Keep a notebook.

Grades 9–12: Foreign Language III

Coming into the class a student should demonstrate ability to:

- Read the language with understanding; translate;
- Participate in simple conversations;
- use idiomatic expressions appropriately;
- Write grammatically correct sentences.

In the class students are taught to:

- Improve accent and intonation when speaking;
- Increase ability to think and converse in the language;

- Add significant numbers of words to active and passive vocabulary; increase idiomatic expressions used actively;
- Improve understanding of and ability to use all verb forms;
- Increase knowledge of the history and culture of the countries for which the language is native;
- Read in the language, for appreciation with and without translation; translate into idiomatic English;
- Translate from English into idiomatic form in language;
- Define words in the language; memorize pieces;
- Write accurately in the language from dictation;
- Compose expository and creative pieces in the language;
- Use colloquial speech patterns when speaking and writing.

Grades 10–12: Foreign Language IV and V

Students taking the fourth and fifth year of a language concentrate on reading the literature, understanding the history and mores of the people using the language in conversation, and in creative and expository writing and improving accent and intonation to the point of being taken for a native speaker.

Both oral and silent reading are encouraged. Students learn to converse fluently in the studied language. They are expected to be able to hear, understand and write whatever they can say.

Opportunity is provided for students to listen to tapes in the studied language, to watch films and to function in the language without translation. Students are expected, as well, to be able to translate from the studied language to English and from English to the studied language with facility, producing a colloquially acceptable product in each language.

Students are also expected to complete expository writing assignments and to produce work in the studied language that is technically correct in use of vocabulary, spelling and grammar.

Chapter 6

HEALTH IN THE CLASSROOM

OVERVIEW

Many states require that health education be taught in every grade. The content will vary somewhat from one school system to another. The grades in which particular topics are covered may also vary and may even overlap as indicated in the secondary school plan shown here.

Some systems include sex education. Others do not. Sex education is included in the curriculum description below.

Grade K—Instruction is provided in: taking care of the body and parts of the body; five senses; good eating and sleeping habits; street safety; germs and cleanliness; drugs and medicines; differences between foods and non-food substances; manners; family relationships.

Grade 1—Instruction is provided in: being a good citizen; manners; sportsmanship; safety in play, on a bicycle, on the street as a pedestrian; care of teeth, eyes, skin, body; shots and medicine; standards of nutrition; elementary first aid; germs; community workers; family responsibilities.

Grade 2—Instruction is provided in: handling illness; hospitals; drugs and medicines; traffic safety; hazards in the environment; cleanliness and body care; nutrition; five main senses and care of the sense organs; the backbone and its function; feelings and managing them; reproduction in lower life forms.

Grade 3—Instruction is provided in: caring for and protecting the body including: permanent teeth, posture, feet, sense organs; nutrition and rest; safety; expressing feelings; germs; drugs and medicine; hazards of alcohol, tobacco and other substances; embryonic development in human and other life forms.

Grade 4—Instruction is provided in: caring for the body; nutrition; first aid for cuts and burns; understanding the body's protective mechanisms; growth timetables; how bones mend; how cuts heal; safety; germs,

53

drugs and medicine; use and abuse of hazardous substances; male and female anatomical differences.

Grade 5—Instruction is provided in: caring for the body; nutrition; effects of substance abuse; function and protection of the brain; blood types; function of blood in the body; drugs and medicines; visual and auditory defects; diseases and medicines; germs; emotional development; male and female body changes during adolescence; menstruation.

Grade 6—Instruction is provided in: grooming; handling emotions in stressful situations; disease and community responsibility; effects of substance abuse; poisons; nutrition; safety; renowned scientists' contribution to health; ecology and pollution; male and female development; human fertilization.

Grade 7—Instruction is provided in: handling stress; mental health; exercise and safety; balancing a diet; understanding body systems including: digestive, dental, nervous, circulatory, endocrine, reproductive; effects of substance and alcohol abuse; pollution and ecology; consumer education; abortion, contraception and right to life; venereal and life-threatening diseases; dating.

Grade 8—Instruction is provided in: the skeletal system and body organs including: kidneys, gallbladder, lungs, heart, liver, bladder; effects of substance abuse; quackery in medicine; first aid and safety; nutrition; exercise; normal pregnancy and potential difficulties; hetero- and homosexuality; sexually transmitted diseases; emotions; steady dating.

Grade 9—Instruction is provided in: recognizing symptoms of illness; first aid; effects of substance abuse; care of body; rest and exercise; nutrition; emotions; sexual diseases; male and female maturation; birth control; child abuse; sexuality in humans; family responsibility; emotional interaction; safety on the street, in the home, on the playing fields.

Grades 10–12: Instruction is provided in: understanding body diseases and treatments including: mono, obesity, anorexia, bulemia, cancer, diabetes, palsy, polio, smallpox, epilepsy, measles, etc.; effects of chronic disease on families; formulas for healthful living; healthy sexual relations; dating; marriage and the community; current social challenges including: child abuse, divorce, remarriage, abortion, birth control, sexual diseases and sexual health, child rearing, old age, death and dying; genetics and personal inheritance; health careers; consumer practices.

Grades 10–12: Instruction is provided in: driver's education; automobile safety; rules of the road; weather and coping with road hazards; insurance; purchasing a car; legal responsibility attached to a car; physical and mental fitness for driving; effects of substance abuse and driving; mechanics of an automobile; family relationships and the car; community relationships and the car; sexual relationships and the car.

HEALTH IN THE CLASSROOM

Grade K

Coming into the grade a student should be able to:

- Take care of his or her own bodily functions;
- Listen, speak and follow directions.

In the grade students are taught:

- The importance of cleanliness and grooming;
- Proper care of the teeth; healthy eating habits;
- The need for medical and dental care;
- Safety on the streets and roads;
- Good eating habits and beneficial foods;
- To understand germs and how they affect us;
- Why the body needs sleep and how much is needed;
- Cautions involving the use of medicine;
- Good manners and why they are important;
- Names of the five senses and how we use them;
- Correct terms for all parts of the body;
- How to get the most benefit from family relationships by giving as well as taking.

Grade 1

Coming into the grade a student should be able to:

- Manage personal cleanliness;
- Know and practice safety rules;
- Understand and use good food and sleep habits and good manners.

In the grade students are taught:

- The importance of physical exercise in keeping fit;
- Simple standards of nutrition and good foods to eat;
- The importance of breakfast;
- Elementary rules of citizenship;
- How to function as a good family member;
- Safety regulations for bicycle riding, crossing, playing;
- Simple first-aid rules;
- To recognize and express emotions;
- How the body reacts to germs, shots, medicine;
- Proper care of teeth, hair, eyes, ears and skin;
- Why we lose baby teeth;
- Why rest and sleep are important to the body;
- The dangers of tobacco and alcohol.

Grade 2

Coming into the grade a student should be able to:

- Discuss safety rules and rules of first aid;
- Demonstrate knowledge of good habits of cleanliness, nutrition, rest, sleep, grooming and manners;
- Talk about feelings and demonstrate consideration for peers and adults.

In the grade students are taught:

- To exercise good judgment when approached by strangers;
- The functions and care of the sense organs, of the five senses (hearing-ears, seeing-eyes, touching-skin, smelling-nose, tasting-mouth);
- Importance of breakfast and good habits of nutrition;
- How the body moves; importance and function of backbone;
- Function of hospitals and how they help us;
- The differences between "drugs" and medicines;

- How to recognize and avoid hazards in the environment;
- How to recognize and manage feelings;
- How some simple plants and animals reproduce.

Grade 3

Coming into the grade a student should be able to:

- Demonstrate knowledge of safety rules, nutrition, manners;
- Discuss the five senses, the sense organs and the backbone;
- Understand some forms of reproduction.

In the grade students are taught:

- Elements of good sportsmanship and good citizenship;
- The importance of exercise to good health;
- The body's need for food and sleep to provide growth;
- Appropriate ways to express feelings; sharing;
- Rules for fire safety and for use of fire;
- Bicycle safety; road and street safety; first aid;
- The difference between reasonable challenges and senseless risks; how to judge danger;
- Care of permanent teeth; care of feet;
- Importance of good posture;
- Hazards of tobacco, alcohol and other drugs;
- How eggs are fertilized and embryos develop.

Grade 4

Coming into the grade a student should be able to:

- Demonstrate knowledge of the importance to good health of nutrition, rest, sleep, cleanliness, safety, exercise, comfort, medicine, consideration for others;
- Discuss fertilization and embryonic development.

In the grade students are taught:

- Individual growth timetables; adapting and adjusting to growth; how bones mend; how cuts heal;
- Food and digestive organs; bodily protective mechanisms;
- Safety at home, in school, in sports and games;
- Dangers of tobacco, alcohol and drugs;
- Personal hygiene practices and good grooming;

- Importance of assuming responsibility at home and in school; importance of understanding peer relationships;
- Male and female anatomical differences;
- How animal are conceived; their pre-natal development.

Grade 5

Coming into the grade a student should be able to:

- Demonstrate understanding of the human body and its functions relative to: sense organs, digestive organs, nutrition, cleanliness, comfort, exercise, rest, drugs, medicines, emotions;
- Demonstrate knowledge of safety, first aid, accepting responsibility and forming healthy peer relationships.

In the grade students are taught:

- Long- and short-range effects of smoke and alcohol on the body;
- The effects of food additives and junk foods;
- Importance of good nutrition to proper body functioning;
- Blood types and their importance to the individual;
- Effects of near- and farsightedness and their control;
- Loss of hearing and coping mechanisms;
- Names and descriptions of some congenital diseases;
- Aspects of male and female maturation; the menstrual cycle;
- Aspects of emotional development; control; handling family and personal stress; use and abuse of medicines and drugs;
- Function and protection of the brain and nervous system;
- Safety and first-aid practices.

Grade 6

Coming into the grade a student should be able to:

- Demonstrate understanding of emotions and emotional control
- Understand the functions of the body and their relation to food, care, exercise, cleanliness and safety;
- Understand male and female development, growth, physical changes, sexual growth, social and emotional needs.

In the grade students are taught:

- The contributions of famous scientists to human health;
- Community roles and responsibility in health care;
- Importance of grooming, exercise and body care;

- Ecology and pollution and what they mean to human health;
- Nature and effect of communicable diseases and venereal diseases; controlling impulses;
- Human fertilization cycles; facts of human conception.

Grade 7

Coming into the grade a student should demonstrate knowledge of:

- Body functions and body structure;
- Good nutrition practices;
- Male and female maturation; facts of human conception;
- History and development of disease control.

In the grade students are taught:

- Appreciation of the role of science and scientists in identifying and solving health problems;
- Long- and short-range effects of nutrition practices;
- Importance to the body of the glands and the endocrine system; how some body systems function (digestive, dental, nervous, circulatory, reproductive); how to deal with skin problems; importance of exercise;
- How diseases affect the body; life-threatening diseases;
- Contraception; right to life; abortion; venereal disease; making choices;
- Effects of tobacco, alcohol and drug use, abuse and misuse;
- Emotional development and dating.

Grade 8

Coming into the grade a student should demonstrate knowledge of:

- Disease and disease control; body systems; good health practices for maturing young people;
- Conception and contraception.

In the grade students are taught:

- The skeletal system, body organs and their functions including: gallbladder, bladder, kidneys, heart, lungs;
- Daily calorie requirements and what burns calories; safety; exercise; good grooming;
- Normal pregnancies and potential difficulties;
- Medicine; quackery; drug and substance abuse;

- Dating; emotions; mental health; sexuality and adjustment;
- Ecology and public health.

Grades 9–10

Coming into the grade a student should demonstrate knowledge of:

- Body systems and organs;
- Personal hygiene, grooming, safety;
- Communicable diseases including venereal diseases;
- Male and female maturation; conception and contraception;
- Tobacco, alcohol and drug abuse.

In the class students are taught:

- Genetic characteristics and how they are transmitted;
- Normal and abnormal functioning of body systems;
- Treatment of those who misuse drugs;
- Recognizing and coping with health problems including: obesity, diabetes, cancer, tuberculosis, mono, epilepsy, bulimia, anorexia, polio, palsy, smallpox, heart disease, high and low blood pressure, high cholesterol;
- Effects on the family of chronic illness, mental and physical handicaps, depression, suicide, sexually transmitted diseases; coping mechanisms;
- Human sexuality, birth control, family responsibility;
- Environmental pollution and ecology;
- Health careers and consumer education.

Grades 10–12

Coming into the class a student should demonstrate:

- Sufficient maturity to be entrusted with control of a car
- Knowledge of the effects of alcohol and drugs on the body

In the class students are taught about:

- Family life-styles; marriage; divorce; living single;
- Child rearing; child abuse;
- Family planning; birth control; abortion; right to life;
- Psychology and physiology of aging and the aged;
- Chronic illness and its effects; sexually transmitted diseases and their effects;
- Exercise, nutrition and body care;

- Death and dying and coping with it;
- Rules of the road for the driver;
- Skills of driving an automobile;
- Physical and mental control needed for safe driving;
- The effect of weather on control of the automobile;
- Insurance coverage for cars and drivers; costs of insurance;
- Basic mechanics of an automobile;
- Family relationships and the car;
- Effects of diseases, nutrition, mental or physical impairment on driving; physical handicaps and driving;
- Responsibility of the driver to the rest of society;
- Consumer education and health careers and opportunities.

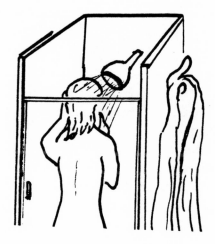

Chapter 7

HOME ECONOMICS IN THE CLASSROOM

OVERVIEW

Home Economics is offered (and in some states required) in the middle grades. Generally, the first offering is in grade seven but may be as early as grade five. The curriculum presented here begins in grade seven.

Offerings in grades nine through twelve are generally electives. A, B, C refers to the sequence of the courses. Both boys and girls, in most school systems, take Home Economics. The courses described below are typical but neither exclusive nor all inclusive.

Grade 7—CLOTHING CONSTRUCTION—(Generally one semester) *Students are instructed in:* sewing machine use and care; use of patterns; selecting fabrics, sizes, seams, fasteners; labels and consumer information; clothing careers.

Grade 7—FOODS—(Generally one semester) *Students are instructed in:* measuring liquid and dry ingredients; following a recipe; basic four food groups; shopping and consumer education; table setting; serving; safety in cooking; sanitation; cleanup; food careers.

Grade 8—CLOTHING—(Generally one semester) *Students are instructed in:* special sewing techniques; following pattern techniques; consumer and career education.

Grade 8—FOODS—(Generally one semester) *Students are instructed in:* balancing a diet; meal planning and preparation; consumer and career education.

Grades 9–12—CLOTHING (A,B,C)—Students are instructed in: methods of recognizing and selecting textiles; natural and man-made fibers; fashion; constructing garments; fabrics and furniture; fabrics and interior decoration; needlecraft; mending; care of clothing; consumer education; careers in textiles and clothing.

Grades 9–12: FOODS AND NUTRITION (A,B,C)—Students are instructed in: menu planning; timing and time-work plans; nutritional content of foods; pastries; yeast doughs; cakes and breads; selecting and cooking meats and fish; salad preparation; vegetables; fruits; ethnic (including regional American) cooking; using milk, eggs, and cheeses; soups; calories; consumer education; food careers.

Grades 11–12: CHILD CARE AND DEVELOPMENT—Students are taught basics of: body growth; cleanliness and physical care; nutrition; behavior patterns; individual differences; mental and emotional development; routines; family life; discipline; nurturing; group interaction; safety; child care careers.

HOME ECONOMICS IN THE CLASSROOM

Grade 7: Clothing and Food

Coming into the class a student should demonstrate ability to:

- Understand and follow written directions;
- Use measuring tools and work in standard and metric;
- Use a scissor for precise cutting.

In the class students are taught to:

- Use and care of a sewing machine;
- Read, interpret and use patterns;
- Create a garment from a pattern;
- Understand methods used when working with different fabrics; identify the grain in a fabric;

- Understand the vocabulary of sewing;
- Use kitchen equipment effectively and safely when cooking;
- Be aware of the importance of sanitation in a kitchen;
- Use appropriate measuring techniques for dry and wet measures;
- Understand the vocabulary of food preparation;
- Use appropriate table-setting and serving techniques;
- Plan a meal using the basic four food groups;
- Prepare and serve: fruit, cereal, eggs, bread, breakfast meat;
- Shop wisely as a consumer.

Grade 8: Clothing and Food

Coming into the class a student should demonstrate ability to:

- Sew a seam; follow and cut a pattern; use a sewing machine;
- Prepare and serve a breakfast.

In the class students are taught to:

- Improve ability to create sewn projects from patterns;
- Sew in zippers, pockets, buttonholes;
- Use appropriate garment care techniques;
- Plan a well-balanced lunch and supper;
- Prepare and serve soups, salads, casseroles, desserts;
- Use appropriate kitchen appliances safely;
- Clean up and observe sanitation rules;
- Be a wise shopper and consumer;
- Become familiar with careers in Home Economics.

Grades 9–12: Textiles (A,B,C)

Coming into the class a student should demonstrate ability to:

- Use a sewing machine to create a project from a pattern;
- Read a pattern.

In the class students are taught to:

- Recognize fabrics;
- Select fabrics appropriate to projects;
- Use sewing machine attachments;
- Include needlecraft skills in planning projects;
- Understand and rely on consumer protection laws;
- Select and use proper techniques for care and preservation of garments;

- Build on skills learned from grade to grade;
- Become familiar with careers available in the field.

Grades 9–12: Foods (A,B,C)

Coming into the class a student should demonstrate ability to:

- Prepare and serve a balanced meal;
- Use proper safety and sanitary methods in the kitchen.

In the class students are taught to:

- Prepare food based on complex menus;
- Develop time-work plans for meal preparation;
- Prepare pastries and yeast doughs;
- Prepare salads, fruits, vegetables;
- Understand "real cost" of items purchased;
- Understand nutritional content of various foods;
- Appreciate and use recipes for foods of different cultures;
- Prepare different foods from regional American cuisine;
- Become familiar with international cuisine;
- Use food supplements and preserve foods;
- Understand use of fats, oils and yeast in food preparation;
- Understand the cuts of meat and fish and their preparation;
- Understand calories and their effects;
- Understand use of convenience foods and jiffy meals;
- Understand good consumer practices;
- Appreciate career opportunities in the field.

Grades 11–12: Child Care and Development

Coming into the class a student should demonstrate ability to:

- Relate with enthusiasm to pre-school children;
- Behave maturely and responsibly.

In the class students are taught:

- Aspects of child development including: behavior patterns, body growth, individual differences, mental and emotional growth;
- Childhood routines including: meals, sleep and rest, play, discipline, family life;
- Children's health and behavior patterns;
- Necessary equipment for child care centers;
- Types of child care facilities available;

- Children's need for affection and acceptance;
- Appropriate activities for pre-school children;
- Safety and care of children;
- Aspects of responsibility necessary for proper child care;
- Child care careers.

Chapter 8

INDUSTRIAL ARTS IN THE CLASSROOM

OVERVIEW

The Industrial Arts offering generally begins in the middle grades, sometimes as early as grade five, but in most school systems in grade seven. Both boys and girls take Industrial Arts. In grades nine through twelve, the offerings are usually elective and sequential.

These are examples of courses which may be offered in a typical American high school. There may be more or fewer in any particular school. The course content will depend on facilities.

Grade 7—SHOP: Students are taught the basics of: shop safety; using tools appropriately; working with metals including: bending, folding, fastening, casting, pouring, forging, machining, boring, tapping, cold forming, wrought iron, finishing, painting and protective coating; working with wood and styrofoam including: safety practices, sawing, fastening with screws, nails, glue; using and understanding power machines; finishing techniques; industrial careers.

Grade 8—SHOP: Students are instructed in: safe use of equipment; three-dimensional drawings; using power machines including: lathe, band saws, drills, sanders; face milling; squaring; angular milling; joining techniques; finishing; project construction; careers.

Grades 9–12—METAL SHOP
Grades 9–12—WOODWORKING SHOP
Grades 9–12—MACHINE SHOP
Grades 9–12—TECHNICAL DRAWING
Grades 9–12—DRAFTING
Grades 9–12—ELECTRICITY AND ELECTRONICS
Grades 9–12—RADIO AND TELEVISION
Grades 9–12—AUTO MECHANICS

INDUSTRIAL ARTS IN THE CLASSROOM

Grade 7: Metals and/or Woods

Coming into the class a student should demonstrate ability to:

- Read, write and follow written directions;
- Handle tools and instruments with care;
- Read and understand measuring devices.

In the class students are taught to:

- Understand and obey safety regulations;
- Layout, bend, fold and fasten metal;
- Use correct techniques for pouring and casting; forging; soldering;
- Do machining, including: filing, boring, tapping;
- Use metal fasteners;
- Identify types of ferrous and non-ferrous metals;
- Operate, identify, and name basic hand and bench tools;
- Identify types and grains of wood;
- Measure and cut wood;
- Fasten wood using nails, screws, dowls, glues;
- Prepare projects for finishing;
- Choose and use appropriate finishing techniques on wood and metal;
- Clean and maintain work area.

Grade 8: Metals and/or Woods

Coming into the class a student should demonstrate ability to:

- Function safely and effectively in a shop setting;
- Read and follow directions.

In the class students are taught to:

- Make three view scale drawings;
- Read a blueprint; work from a scale drawing;
- Do face milling, squaring and angular milling;
- Prepare metal and braze using oxyacetylene;
- Accomplish variety of joining methods in wood including: dado, tongue in groove, rabbet, miter, dowel; glue and clamp; use of a lathe;
- Compute costs of projects;
- Understand concepts of industrial products and processes;
- Use a variety of finishes on metal and wood;

- Explore career possibilities in the Industrial Arts;
- Understand good consumer practices.

Grades 9-12: Woodworking

Coming into the class a student should demonstrate ability to:

- Do basic drafting, drawing and planning;
- Handle power tools safely.

In the class students are taught to:

- Use table saw to crosscut and rip stock; cut miters, tenons; mortises; splines; angles; resaw stock;
- Join edges; bevel; chamfer; tape;
- Use a drill press and jigs;
- Shape molding; cut curved and irregular surfaces and edges;
- Use saber saw and cut scrolls and patterns; plunge cut;
- Use router and cut: gains; dado; moldings; dovetail;
- Maintain tools, machines and work area;
- Understand and obey safety regulations;
- Find out about career options in the field.

Grades 9-12: Metals

Coming into the class a student should demonstrate ability to:

- Do basic drafting, drawing and planning;
- Handle tools safely.

In the class students are taught:

- Sheet metal safety;
- Industrial applications of sheet metal skills;
- Use of sheet metal tools: hand tools; layout tools; power tools; measuring tools (standard and metric);
- Drill press theory and operation;
- Squaring-shear theory and operation;
- Fasteners: soldering; riveting; steaming;
- Drafting and pattern development;
- Sheet metal finishes and application methods;
- Sheet metal mathematics;
- Careers in sheet metal trades.

Grades 9–12: Machine Shop

Coming into the class a student should demonstrate ability to:

- Function safely and with knowledge in a sheet metal shop;
- Plan and create projects.

In the class students are taught:

- Engine lathe theory and operation;
- Milling machine theory and operation;
- Grinder operation;
- Metalurgy;
- Heat treating;
- Machine shop mathematics;
- Machinability of metals;
- Production turning: theory and operation;
- Numerical control of machines;
- Robotic control of machines;
- Availability of careers in machine trades.

Grades 9–12: Electricity and Electronics

Coming into the class a student should demonstrate ability to:

- Comprehend applied mathematical and algebraic principles;
- Ability to read with comprehension;
- Ability to follow detailed instructions.

In the class students are taught:

- Atomic theory;
- Sources of electricity; power supplies;
- AC and DC applications;
- Laws and effects of magnetism;
- Inductance and RL circuits; and RC circuits;
- Tuned circuits; electron tubes;
- Transistors; integrated circuits; complex circuits;
- Amplifiers, receivers and transmitters;

- Use of meters and scopes;
- Career opportunities in the electronics field.

Grades 9–12: *Technical Drawing*

Coming into the class a student should demonstrate ability to:

- Function with basic mathematical concepts;
- Read a ruler; interpret meaning of fractions and decimals.

In the class students are taught:

- Orthographic projections: multi-view; dimensioning; sectioning; auxiliary views; revolutions; rotations;
- Pictorial drawings;
- Sheet metal development;
- Intersections;
- Machine drawing;
- Threads and fasteners; cams; gears; bearings and bushings;
- Jigs and fixtures;
- Detail and assembly machine drawings;
- Applying of principles of geometric construction;
- Reading a blueprint.

Grades 9–12: *Architectural Drafting*

Coming into the class a student should demonstrate ability to:

- Handle drafting tools;
- Understanding basic mathematics and measuring concepts.

In the class students are taught:

- Construction principles
- Planning and layout for heating, plumbing, electricity;
- Specifications:
- Cost analysis, building costs, financing;

- Importance of neatness and accuracy;
- Career opportunities in the field of architecture.

Chapter 9

LANGUAGE ARTS IN THE CLASSROOM

OVERVIEW

Reading, writing, listening and speaking in the English language are the basic tools of communication and the focal skills of what schools call the Language Arts. These are known under a variety of names from English to Communications and are taught in every school grade from kindergarten through twelve. In each grade instructional focus is on reading, writing listening and speaking.

Grade K—Instruction is provided in:

READING: Recognizing letters; left to right eye and hand movement; putting pictures in order; decoding; memorizing; handling books;

WRITING: Tracing and forming letters; dictating stories; using a computer keyboard; crayoning;

LISTENING: Following verbal directions; discriminating sounds; understanding stories; interacting with peers;

SPEAKING: Telling things to peers and adults; increasing vocabulary; expressing ideas; recalling details; analyzing.

Grade 1—Instruction is provided in:

READING: Recognizing and naming letters of the alphabet; recognizing and building word families; developing a sight vocabulary; matching; putting letters of the alphabet, words, pictures and parts of stories in correct order; responding appropriately to written directions; reading silently and aloud on a pre-primer, primer and book one level with understanding; reading simple story books for enjoyment;

WRITING: Forming the letters of the alphabet in manuscript; using letters to make and spell words correctly; making up simple sentences; copying; using a computer keyboard;

LISTENING: Recognizing same and different sounds; using phonics to sound out words; identifying synonyms, antonyms, homonyms;

identifying beginning, middle and ending sounds; using rhyming words; understanding and following directions;

SPEAKING: Asking and answering questions; conversing; memorizing and reciting; summarizing, telling and retelling stories.

Grade 2—Instruction is provided in:

READING: Decoding; increasing sight vocabulary; phonics; using the dictionary; reading with understanding book two in the reading series; introduction to literature; improving sequencing skills; defining and analyzing words; using correct grammar; synonyms, antonyms, homonyms; using the library;

WRITING: Creative writing of sentences and paragraphs; spelling; writing from dictation; editing; capitalization and punctuation; letter writing; correct formation and spacing of letters in manuscript; using a computer;

LISTENING: Responding appropriately to oral directions; analyzing and critiquing oral reports and stories;

SPEAKING: Memorizing and reciting; conversing; making a point; making an oral report; speaking in sentences.

Grade 3—Instruction is provided in:

READING: Decoding; extending sight vocabulary; phonics; dictionary skills; glossary; table of contents; book three in reading series; use of library for reference and literature; reading aloud to inform and entertain; reading for information; reading with comprehension;

WRITING: Composing letters, postcards and addressing envelopes; writing to inform; creative writing; reports; spelling, grammar and dictation; introduction to cursive writing; using a computer;

LISTENING: Following directions; taking notes; hearing and responding to oral presentation of content material;

SPEAKING: Conversing; grammatical use of the language when speaking; using sentences; memorizing and reciting; oral reporting; convincing.

Grade 4—Instruction is provided in:

READING: Decoding, defining and analyzing new words; comprehending; identifying main idea; finding details; critically evaluating; book four in reader; increasing vocabulary; study skills; fluent reading aloud; use of reference books in library and classroom; reading for content; reading literature for appreciation;

WRITING: Creative and factual composition; reports; spelling rules; rules of grammar, punctuation, capitalization; improved control of cursive writing; outlining; writing from dictation; use of computer;

LISTENING: Critical listening; taking notes; listening for content and remembering; following oral directions;

SPEAKING: Conversing; presenting ideas and information fluently; using standard pronunciation; memorizing and reciting; convincing.

Grade 5—Instruction is provided in:

READING: Decoding and vocabulary development; interpreting characterization; recognizing differences between fact and opinion; skillful use of reference materials; extracting information; book five in reader; reading literature for comprehension, enjoyment and appreciation; using library; reading aloud to inform and entertain;

WRITING: Applying grammatical and spelling rules to creative and expository writing; using proper paragraphing, word order, punctuation and capitalization; outlining, taking notes and writing reports; cursive writing practice; using a computer and/or a typewriter;

LISTENING: Aurally obtaining content from oral presentation; conversing; following directions; convincing; distinguishing standard speech patterns from regionalisms;

SPEAKING: Memorizing and reciting; pronunciation; expanded vocabulary; presenting an argument; accurately relaying a message.

Grade 6—Instruction is provided in:

READING: Increasing comprehension and appreciation; using the library; expanding vocabulary; figures of speech, imagery, idioms; improving reading speed; fluent oral reading; book six in reader; reading for information; reading literature;

WRITING: Control of cursive writing skills; creating short stories, poetry, reports; spelling and grammar rules; note taking; outlining; capitalization, punctuation, paragraph forming; using a computer;

LISTENING: Taking notes; obtaining content from oral presentations; following directions; conversing;

SPEAKING: convincing; presenting information concisely; memorizing and reciting; expanded vocabulary; accurate reporting.

In the secondary grades students are expected to do intensive literary reading. Each school system determines the grades in which it will concentrate on a particular type of literature, but during the secondary school years students will, in one grade or another, read Shakespeare, American literature, British literature, literature in translation from foreign languages, poetry, the novel and plays. The pattern of offerings below is typical.

Grade 7—Instructional focus is on: recognizing and using basic sentence patterns; using proper grammar forms; verbs, nouns, pronouns, adjectives, adverbs, prepositions, conjunctions, interjections; punctuating correctly; expanding reading and oral vocabulary and ability to define words; spelling correctly and using spelling rules; improving speaking ability, intonation, pronunciation; library reference skills; creating and using bibliographies; creative and expository writing; note taking and outlining; proofreading; brainstorming; summarizing; memorizing; reciting; reading literary selections; using the library for pleasure and research; using a computer.

Grade 8—Instructional focus is on: understanding and expanding sentence patterns; writing paragraphs; simple and compound sentences; improving handwriting; using verb and noun forms correctly; possessives; spelling; precis; outlining and summarizing; proofreading; finding main ideas and supporting details; comprehending; evaluating speeches and speech outlines; reading and appreciating Greek and Roman myths; studying selected novels, plays and poems; reading selected autobiographies and biographies; brainstorming; independent reading; developing a literary memory; using a computer.

Grade 9—Instructional focus is on: using and understanding gerunds, infinitives, participles and clauses; using figurative and imaginative language; paragraph and style; coherence; outlining; formal elements of short stories, novels, drama, novelettes: introduction to Shakespeare and his work and times; plays; analogies; analysis of literary characters; comprehending; use of evidence in writing speeches; creative and expository writing; scholarly use of the library; expanding vocabulary; use of computer.

Grade 10—Instructional focus is on: paragraph development; using logical progression in speaking and writing; cause-and-effect relationships; critiquing; figures of speech; simile and metaphor; vocabulary and analogies; connotation; denotation; comprehension; precis writing; effective sentences and paragraphs; survey of American literature and writers; styles in literature; drawing inferences; images; grammar and writing forms; note taking and outlining; scholarly use of the library; use of computer.

Grade 11—Instructional focus is on: increasing student vocabulary control; correct usage in writing and speaking; working with analogies; improving writing through sentence integrity, coordination, subordination, transition, parallelism; research skills for written term papers; bibliography; essay; footnoting; satire and allegory; critiquing; effective public speaking; note taking and outlining; survey of British literature in historical and literary context; use of the library for research and enjoyment; use of a computer.

Grade 12—Instructional focus is on: distinguishing multiple meanings of words; analogies; applying tools of literary criticism; developing objectivity, critical judgment, and taste; expository writing techniques; intensive review of grammar and usage skills; writing a term paper, bibliography, footnoting; reading for information and enjoyment the literature in translation from other languages (Russian, German, Spanish, French); comprehension; use of computer.

Additional offerings in the secondary school Language Arts curriculum may include electives such as the following:

- Poetry
- Film
- Shakespeare (Comedies, Tragedies, Sonnets)
- Drama Workshop
- Theater Arts
- Journalism
- Creative Writing
- Remedial English
- Literature in Translation
- Speech
- Poetry and Poets
- The Theory of Knowledge
- Great Books
- Humanities

LANGUAGE ARTS IN THE CLASSROOM

Grade K

Coming into the grade a student should be able to:

- Listen with understanding and follow directions;
- Speak in sentences;
- Recognize *some* symbols (letters of alphabet, some words)

In the grade students are taught to:

- Identify letters (capital and small), words, sounds, sentences;
- Match objects and pictures; tell what's happening in pictures;
- Listen to and enjoy stories, poems, riddles, jokes; act out stories; recite rhymes;
- Write letters of the alphabet (capital and small); match capital and small letters; follow text from left to right, top to bottom, front to back of book;
- Recognize (read) own name; write own name;
- Hold pencil correctly and sit properly when writing;
- Identify consonant sounds at beginning and end of a word;

- Hear and repeat exactly a five-word sentence;
- Relate a sequence of events; listen with comprehension;
- Recall and relate major ideas of story; speak in sentences;
- Classify objects and pictures (toys, foods, clothes, etc.);
- Trace letters with a finger, a pencil; copy letters;
- Dictate a story to be written by an older person;
- Become familiar with a computer keyboard.

Grade 1

Coming into the grade a student should be able to:

- Listen, speak in sentences and follow directions;
- Identify beginning and final sounds of words;
- Put stories in sequential order and interpret them;
- Write upper- and lowercase manuscript letters while holding a pencil properly and sitting with good posture.

In the grade students are taught to:

- Identify words using initial and final letter cues;
- Hear and see same sounds in different words; read word families (at, end, etc.); recognize words and develop a sight vocabulary; read and understand the words in the pre-primer, primer and first grade book of the reading series;
- Use elementary decoding skills to read words;
- Use pictures, context clues and word-attack skills;
- Retell and act out events in a story; tell a story; tell a book report; select an appropriate name for a story;
- Read orally and silently with comprehension and without lip movement;
- Distinguish between reality and fantasy;
- Classify and sequence pictures and words;
- Use correct forms of is-are, went-gone, did-done, saw-seen, has-have, I-me;
- Recognize difference between telling and asking sentences;
- Follow printed instructions; respond to oral instructions;
- Read, trace and write all letters in manuscript;
- Write simple sentences; correct spelling and punctuation;
- Recognize, name, and use letters on the computer keyboard;
- Spell words using spelling patterns, memorizing skills, order of sounds and rhyming skills;

- Use a simple dictionary to find words by the first letter;
- Copy material from the board;
- Recognize differences in words: opposites (antonyms), words spelled alike with different meanings (homographs), words which sound alike but have different spellings (homophones);
- Ask and answer questions; converse with peers and adults;
- Speak in sentences using standard speech patterns.

Grade 2

Coming into the grade a student should be able to:

- Demonstrate grade level reading and comprehension skills;
- Name and write letters of the alphabet and simple sentences;
- Spell and punctuate correctly;
- Communicate ideas clearly; tell stories about things.

In the grade students are taught to:

- Use decoding skills, context clues, picture clues to read words; expand sight vocabulary; words in grade reader;
- Retell, retitle, and act out events in a story;
- Memorize and recite selected poems;
- Read orally with comprehension and correct phrasing;
- Read silently for information and enjoyment without lip movement; distinguish between reality and fantasy;
- Classify and sequence pictures and words; use index and table of contents; alphabetize words to second letter; use a dictionary;
- Write simple paragraphs; a friendly letter; an envelope;
- Practice manuscript-writing skills; write legibly;
- Write descriptions, stories, poems; book reports;
- Capitalize correctly; punctuate correctly using the period, comma, apostrophe, question mark; use spelling clues and rules; practice spelling words; write words in sentences from dictation; proofread; write simple sentences;
- Follow printed instructions; respond to oral instructions
- Recognize, name and use letters on the computer keyboard;
- Copy material from the board correctly; keep a notebook;
- Recognize difference in words: opposites (antonyms), words spelled alike but with different meanings (homographs), words that sound alike with different spellings (homophones), words with similar meanings (synonyms);

- Ask and answer questions; converse with peers and adults; speak in sentences using standard speech patterns;
- Use parts of speech correctly (noun-verb agreement, pronouns, adjectives, prepositions);
- Evaluate own work and work of others;
- Use good techniques in taking tests;
- Use the library and present oral book reports.

Grade 3

Coming into the grade a student should be able to:

- Read orally with fluency; read with comprehension;
- Use decoding skills for new words;
- Write simple paragraphs with correct spelling and punctuation;
- Write manuscript legibly and neatly.

In the grade students are taught to:

- Use decoding skills, context clues, picture clues to read;
- Expand sight vocabulary to include words in grade reader;
- Participate in vocabulary-building activities;
- Read to recall facts and information, for main idea, for inference; read silently without lip movement; read for enjoyment; report orally and in writing on books read;
- Retell, retitle and act out events in a story; tell a story;
- Memorize and recite selected poems;
- Read orally with correct phrasing and voice intonation;
- Classify and sequence pictures and words; use index and table of contents; use dictionary and glossary to define; to spell;
- Write to inform, to report; friendly letter, envelope, postcard; write descriptions, stories, poems; write an outline;
- Practice cursive writing; compare letters to manuscript;
- Punctuate and capitalize correctly;
- Use spelling clues and rules; spell words on grade list;
- Write spelling words in sentences from dictation; proofread;
- Follow printed instructions; respond to oral instructions;
- Copy material from the board correctly; keep a notebook;
- Recognize difference in words: opposites (antonyms), words spelled alike but with different meanings (homographs), sound alike words with different spellings (homophones), words with similar meanings (synonyms); use analogies;

- Ask and answer questions; converse; make a point; use standard speech patterns; use parts of speech correctly (noun-verb agreement, pronouns, adjectives, prepositions, modifiers, proper nouns);
- Evaluate own work and work of others; take notes;
- Use appropriate techniques in taking tests;
- Use a computer for reinforcing skills; for writing;
- Use the library for information and pleasure.

Grade 4

Coming into the grade a student should be able to:

- Use decoding skills when meeting new words; read silently and aloud with comprehension from third grade readers;
- Write statements, stories and poems in manuscript and cursive forms;
- Spell, punctuate and use grammar correctly;
- Speak in cohesive sentences; converse.

In the grade students are taught to:

- Use decoding and encoding skills, context clues, phonics, for word attack;
- Understand cause-and-effect relationships;
- Expand sight vocabulary to include words in grade reader;
- Sharpen vocabulary-building skills; use dictionary and word-analysis methods; understand value of prefixes and suffixes;
- Read to recall facts and information, main idea; read for inference; read silently, without lip movement; read for enjoyment; make oral and written book reports;
- Retell, retitle and act out events in a story; tell a story;
- Memorize and recite selected poems and literary passages;
- Read orally with correct phrasing and voice intonation;
- Use index and table of contents; use dictionary for spelling, defining and pronunciation; use a glossary and an encyclopedia;
- Write to inform: a report, a friendly letter, an envelope, a postcard; write descriptions, stories, poems; write an outline; use cursive form; write legibly with correct slant; punctuate and capitalize correctly; proofread;
- Spell words on grade list; spell and use possessives;
- Write spelling words in sentences from dictation;
- Memorize and use spelling and grammar rules;

- Recognize differences in words: opposites (antonyms), synonyms, homographs, homophones; use analogies;
- Use parts of speech correctly in speaking and writing: noun-verb agreement, adjectives, adverbs, prepositions, modifiers, proper nouns, subjects, predicates, objects, articles;
- Follow printed instructions; respond to oral instructions;
- Ask and answer questions; converse; make a point; use standard speech patterns;
- Copy material from the board correctly; keep a notebook;
- Evaluate own work and work of others; take notes;
- Use appropriate techniques in taking tests;
- Use a computer for reinforcing skills; for writing;
- Use the library for information and pleasure.

Grade 5

Coming into the grade a student should be able to:

- Read independently for information and enjoyment;
- Use decoding skills on unfamiliar words;
- Write legibly with correct grammar, spelling, punctuation;
- Speak fluently and correctly; use reference materials.

In the grade students are taught to:

- Use decoding and encoding skills, context clues, phonics, for word attack; expand sight vocabulary;
- Sharpen vocabulary-building skills; use a dictionary and word-analysis techniques; use prefixes and suffixes;
- Read for comprehension and inference; factual recall;
- Read silently without lip movement; read for appreciation;
- Read orally with correct phrasing and voice intonation;
- Retell, retitle and act out events in a story; tell a story;
- Memorize and recite selected poems and literary passages;
- Use index and table of contents; dictionary for definitions, spelling and pronunciation; use glossary and encyclopedia;
- Write to inform or report (expository); write dialogue using quotation marks and commas correctly; write a story, a business letter, poems, book reports;
- Practice study skills including outlining, note taking, keep a notebook; use bibliographies, encyclopedia, library reference materials; use library for formal and informal reading; use a dictionary;

- Use cursive form; write legibly with correct slant;
- Punctuate and capitalize correctly; proofread;
- Spell words on grade list; write sentences from dictation;
- Memorize and use spelling and grammar rules;
- Recognize differences in words: synonyms, antonyms, homographs, homophones; use analogies;
- Use parts of speech correctly in speaking and writing: noun-verb agreement, pronoun, linking verb; adjective, adverbs, preposition, proper noun, article, possessive, conjunction;
- Understand sentence structure (subject, predicate, direct object, indirect object, prepositional phrase, word order);
- Identify types of sentences (declarative, interrogative, imperative, exclamatory) and punctuate appropriately;
- Study paragraph structure (topic sentence, main idea);
- Ask and answer questions; converse; make points; convince;
- Use appropriate techniques in taking tests;
- Use a computer for reinforcing skills; for writing.

Grade 6

Coming into the grade a student should be able to:

- Read skillfully orally and silently with comprehension;
- Write and speak grammatically; spell correctly;
- Write multiple-sentence paragraphs;
- Demonstrate command of good study skills.

In the grade students are taught to:

- Use encoding and decoding skills, context clues, phonics, for word attack; sharpen vocabulary-building skills; use a dictionary; word-analysis techniques; prefixes and suffixes;
- Read for comprehension and inference; cause and effect;
- Practice factual recall; find main idea; summarize;
- Read silently without lip movement; read for appreciation;
- Read orally with correct phrasing and voice intonation;
- Use index and table of contents; use dictionary for spelling and pronunciation; use glossary; use encyclopedia;
- Write to inform or report (expository); write dialogue using quotation marks and commas; write business letters, stories (narrative), poems (all forms); book reports;
- Practice study skills including outlining, note taking; keep a notebook;

use bibliographies; library reference materials; use library for formal and informal reading;
- Use cursive form; practice writing legibly;
- Punctuate and capitalize correctly; proofread;
- Spell words on grade list; write sentences from dictation;
- Memorize and use spelling and grammar rules;
- Use antonyms, homographs, homophones, synonyms; analogies;
- Use parts of speech correctly in speaking and writing: noun-verb agreement, pronoun, linking verb; adjective, adverb, prepositions, proper noun, article, possessive, conjunctions; avoid sentence fragments;
- Understand sentence structure: subject, predicate, direct object, indirect object, prepositional phrase, word order,
- Identify, use and punctuate sentences: declarative, interrogative, imperative, exclamatory, compound;
- Paragraph structure: topic sentence, main idea, sequence;
- Identify and use idioms, figures of speech, affixes;
- Participate in group discussions; converse; make points;
- Use appropriate techniques in taking tests;
- Use a computer for reinforcing skills; for writing;
- Read from a prescribed list of books.

In the secondary grades students do extensive reading of literature. The particular grades in which specific assignments are made vary from one system to another. Nevertheless, during the secondary school years students read Shakespeare, American literature, British literature, foreign literature from various countries (in translation), poetry, the novel and plays. The descriptions below reflect one of the patterns in which these courses are offered.

Grade 7

Coming into the class a student should demonstrate ability to:

- Read skillfully with comprehension and appreciation;
- Write clearly using correct grammar, spelling and punctuation;
- Listen effectively for information and enjoyment;
- Speak intelligibly; use study skills effectively.

In the class students are taught to:

- Read and discuss content and style of a variety of literary selections from a prescribed reading list; read poetry and short stories; improve oral reading skills;

- Create and use a bibliography; develop appreciation and taste; write critiques of assigned literary selections;
- Recognize authors; styles; analyze characters; discuss plots; memorize passages;
- Outline; take notes; summarize; practice study skills; keep a notebook; use a dictionary, encyclopedia and library reference materials; use library for formal and informal reading;
- Understand correct grammatical use and function of nouns (all forms), pronouns (all forms), verbs (all tenses and forms), adjectives, adverbs, prepositions, conjunctions, articles, interjections; memorize spelling and grammar rules; spell, capitalize and punctuate correctly;
- Expand vocabulary; use analogies; define and analyze words;
- Participate in expository and creative writing assignments;
- Improve handwriting and proofreading skills;
- Improve formal and informal speaking skills;
- Recognize relationship of ideas; cause and effect;
- Use parts of speech correctly in speaking and writing: noun-verb agreement, linking verbs; adjectives, adverbs, proper nouns, prepositions, articles, possessives, conjunctions, pronouns;
- Understand sentence structure (subject, predicate, direct object, indirect object, prepositional phrases, word order; understand paragraph structure: topic sentence, main idea, sequence;
- Identify types of sentences: compound, complex, declarative, interrogative, imperative, exclamatory;
- Use appropriate techniques in taking tests;
- Use a computer for reinforcing skills; for writing.

Grade 8

Coming into the class a student should demonstrate ability to:

- Read skillfully with comprehension and appreciation;
- Write clearly using correct grammar, spelling and punctuation;
- Listen effectively for information and enjoyment;
- Speak intelligibly; use study skills effectively.

In the class students are taught to:

- Read and discuss content of Greek and Roman myths, selected

fables, biographies, autobiographies, essays, novels, short stories; write reports and summaries of these;
- Improve oral reading skills; memorize passages;
- Recognize authors; styles; analyze characters; discuss plots; read critically; paraphrase;
- Outline; take notes; summarize; write precis; practice study skills; keep a notebook; use encyclopedia and library reference materials; use library for formal and informal reading; write reports; brainstorm;
- Understand correct grammatical use and function of nouns (all forms), pronouns, verbs (all tenses and forms), adjectives, adverbs, prepositions, conjunctions, articles, interjections;
- Use correct spelling, capitalization and punctuation;
- Expand vocabulary; use analogies; define and analyze words;
- Participate in expository and creative writing assignments;
- Improve the quality of written sentences and paragraphs;
- Improve handwriting and proofreading skills;
- Improve formal and informal speaking skills;
- Recognize relationship of ideas; cause and effect;
- Use cursive form and write legibly with correct slant;
- Memorize and use spelling and grammar rules;
- Use parts of speech correctly in speaking and writing: noun-verb agreement, linking verbs; adjectives, adverbs, proper nouns, prepositions, articles, posessives, conjunctions;
- Understand sentence structure: subject, predicate, direct object, indirect object, prepositional phrase, word order;
- Identify types of sentences: compound, declarative, complex, interrogative, imperative, exclamatory; punctuate correctly;
- Review paragraph structure: topic sentence, main idea, sequence;
- Develop appreciation for literature and literary taste;
- Read newspapers and discuss current events;
- Use appropriate techniques in taking tests;
- Use a computer for reinforcing skills; for writing.

Grade 9

Coming into the class a student should demonstrate ability to:

- Discuss aspects of Greek and Roman mythology;
- Identify characteristics of biography and autobiography;
- Write, using correct form, spelling, grammar and punctuation: a

precis, a business and a friendly letter, an expository statement, a creative composition, a poem;

- Take notes during a lecture; listen and glean information;
- Present a point of view in an oral address.

In the class students are taught to:

- Analyze themes in literature; read selected short stories and novels; discuss backgrounds and techniques of authors;
- Read, discuss and dramatize selected works of Shakespeare; memorize selected passages; write a commentary on selected parts of a Shakespearean play;
- Generalize, judge and draw conclusions and inferences from assigned reading;
- Increase understanding of societies and their mores;
- Use literary analysis skills; relate characters to life;
- Write technically correct compositions with clarity and depth; improve paragraph cohesion in writing;
- Outline, take notes, and employ good study habits;
- Improve command of expanding vocabulary;
- Use reference books and materials in the library;
- Recognize and use analogies, idioms, and colloquialisms;
- Improve handwriting and proofreading skills;
- Improve formal and informal speaking skills;
- Recognize relationship of ideas; cause and effect;
- Memorize and use spelling and grammar rules;
- Review noun-verb agreement, verbs, adverbs, adjectives, phrases, prepositions, proper nouns, articles, possessives, pronouns, conjunctions, infinitives, gerunds, participles, clauses; review paragraph structure;
- Read newspapers and discuss current events;
- Use appropriate techniques in taking tests;
- Use a computer for reinforcing skills; for writing.

Grade 10

Coming into the class a student should demonstrate ability to:

- Discuss Shakespearean drama and books read in grade nine;
- Use correct form, spelling, grammar, punctuation; write a precis, a literary commentary, an essay, a creative composition, a poem; relate literary characters to life;

- Take notes during a lecture; listen and glean information;
- Present a point of view in an oral address; recite.

In the class students are taught to:

- Understand and appreciate American literature; read works of representative American authors; discuss the works read in terms of the time and place in which they were written;
- Analyze themes; read selected American short stories and novels; discuss backgrounds and techniques of authors;
- Generalize; judge and draw conclusions and inferences from readings; recognize styles and emerging forms;
- Understand difference between denotation and connotation;
- Develop literary-analysis skills; use inductive and deductive reasoning;
- Evaluate story situations and character action in terms of societal expectations and values;
- Recognize and understand the concept and use of propaganda;
- Write technically correct compositions with clarity and depth; outline; take notes; use good study habits;
- Expand vocabulary; use figure of speech, simile, metaphor;
- Make scholarly use of reference materials; use library;
- Use a bibliography; use the proper form for footnotes;
- Recognize and use analogies, idioms, and colloquialisms;
- Understand techniques used in researching and writing a term paper; write a term paper; write a precis;
- Improve handwriting and proofreading skills;
- Improve formal and informal speaking skills; use supporting data to prove a point; memorize and recite;
- Review noun-verb agreement, verbs, adverbs, adjectives, phrases, prepositions, proper nouns, articles, possessives, pronouns, conjunctions, infinitives, gerunds, participles, clauses; paragraph structure; topic sentences;
- Increase understanding and appreciation of literature;
- Read newspapers and discuss current events;
- Use appropriate techniques in taking tests;
- Use a computer for reinforcing skills; for writing.

Grade 11

Coming into the class a student should demonstrate ability to:

- Discuss aspects of American literature and books read in grades nine and ten;
- Write, using correct grammar and punctuation, spelling and form: precis, a literary commentary, an essay, a creative composition, a poem; write relating literary characters to life;
- Take notes during a lecture; listen and glean information;
- Present a point of view in an oral address; recite.

In the class students are taught to:

- Increase writing effectiveness; use coordination, subordination, transition, parallelism, idioms, coherence;
- Write correct compositions with clarity and depth;
- Outline, take notes and employ good study habits;
- Understand and appreciate British literature from the early Middle Ages to modern times; note the changes in the language, literary styles, mores and values as revealed in the literature; discuss works read in terms of historical context; analyze themes; read selected short stories and British novels; discuss backgrounds and techniques of authors; discuss taste; generalize; draw conclusions and inferences from assigned reading;
- Study fictional and non-fictional forms; note elements of allegory, satire; read poetry, prose, essays, drama;
- Develop literary analysis skills; deduction and induction;
- Evaluate story situations and character action in terms of societal expectations and values;
- Relate British literature to American literature;
- Recognize and understand concept and use of propaganda;
- Improve command of expanding vocabulary; study etymology;
- Make scholarly use of reference materials in the library;
- Develop and use a bibliography; use proper footnote form;
- Recognize and use analogies, similes, metaphors;
- Understand techniques used in researching and writing a term paper; write a reasearch paper; document ideas presented;
- Improve handwriting and proofreading skills;
- Improve formal and informal speaking skills;
- Use supporting data to prove a point; memorize and recite;

- Review all learned aspects of formal grammar;
- Review paragraph structure;
- Read newspapers and discuss current events;
- Use appropriate techniques in taking tests;
- Use a computer for reinforcing skills; for writing.

Grade 12

Coming into the class a student should demonstrate ability to:

- Discuss aspects of American and British literature and books read in grades nine, ten and eleven;
- Write, using correct spelling, grammar and punctuation: a precis, a literary commentary, an essay, a creative composition, a poem; write relating literary characters to one another and to life;
- Take notes during a lecture; listen and glean information;
- Present a point of view in an oral address; recite.

In the class students are taught to:

- Read, understand and appreciate literature translated from other languages (Spanish, Russian, German, French, Italian, Japanese, Chinese, Other) and discuss the times and cultures in which the authors lived and wrote; use tools of literary criticism; analyze themes; discuss backgrounds and methods of authors; generalize and draw conclusions and inferences from reading;
- Study fictional and non-fictional forms; note elements of allegory, satire; read poetry, prose, essays, drama;
- Improve literary-analysis skill; deduction and induction;
- Evaluate story situations and character action in terms of societal expectations and values; develop taste;
- Discuss philosophies and ideas presented in the literature;
- Expand vocabulary; study etymology of words; appreciate and distinguish among multiple connotations and denotations:
- Recognize and understand concept and use of propaganda;
- Improve writing; use coordination, subordination, idioms, transition, parallelism, coherence;
- Write technically correct compositions;
- Outline; take notes; use good study habits;
- Make scholarly use of reference materials; use library;
- Develop and use a bibliography; use proper footnote form;
- Recognize and use analogies, similes, metaphors;

- Understand techniques used in researching and writing a term paper; write a reasearch paper; document ideas presented;
- Improve handwriting and proofreading skills;
- Improve formal and informal speaking skills; use supporting data to prove a point; memorize and recite;
- Review grammatical rules, parts of speech, sentence and paragraph structure, spelling rules, punctuation rules;
- Read newspapers and discuss current events;
- Use appropriate techniques in taking tests;
- Use a computer for reinforcing skills; for writing.

Chapter 10

MATHEMATICS IN THE CLASSROOM

OVERVIEW

Computation skills are taught in every grade, although during some secondary school years students may elect to take other subjects rather than math. Most school systems require at least two years of math in the secondary grades.

The grades in which particular math courses are offered after grade six differ from one system to another. *Beginning in Grade seven math courses are named rather than ascribed to a grade.*

Grade K—Instructional focus is on: understanding number concepts through ten; recognizing numerals through ten; correctly copying numerals; understanding the concepts of taller, shorter, longer, larger, smaller; recognizing shapes and matching them to their names; counting through twenty; naming and valuing coins; using calendars and watches; using computers for simple tasks.

Grade 1—Instructional focus is on: recognizing, writing and putting numbers in correct order up to number 50; addition and subtraction processes; immediate response on number facts of single-digit numbers; solving addition and subtraction problems; recognizing and naming shapes; comparative sizes; metric measurement; telling time in half hours; counting by ones, twos, fives, and tens; value of coins; concept of half; reading digital clock; calendar; using computer and calculator.

Grade 2—Instructional focus is on: writing, ordering, and comparing numbers to 999; adding and subtracting two-digit numbers with and without carrying (regroup); immediate response on number facts of addition and subtraction; solving number problems; dealing with time in minutes, hours, days, weeks, months, years, centuries; using standard and metric measures; understanding symmetry of shapes; using bar, picture and line graphs; reading maps; making change with coins; using number line; estimating to nearest tenth; balancing equations; using a computer and a calculator.

Grade 3—Instructional focus is on: adding and subtracting multiple-digit numbers with carrying; using number line; reading, writing, ordering and comparing numbers to 1,000; understanding that multiplication is repeated addition; division is repeated subtraction; multiplication and division facts with immediate response; fractions and mixed numbers; decimal concepts; time and calendar; metric and standard measures; reading, interpreting and constructing graphs and maps; solving number problems; estimating; identifying shapes; using money for purchasing goods and services; solving equations; using a computer and a calculator.

Grade 4—Instructional focus is on: adding, subtracting, multiplying and dividing multiple-digit numbers with carrying; solving number problems; reading, writing and comparing numbers to millions; place value; estimating; immediate response on number facts; rounding numbers to nearest tenth, hundreth, thousandth; metric measures; perimeter, shapes, angles, length; fractions; decimals; tables, graphs, maps, charts; money concepts to nearest dollar and ten dollars; Roman numerals; equations; using computer and calculator.

Grade 5—Instructional focus is on: using the four basic operations $(+, -, \times, \div)$ on multiple-digit numbers; immediate response on number facts; estimating and rounding results; solving problems; understanding identity elements (0, 1); least common multiple; greatest common factor; operations on fractions and decimals; average; horizontal, vertical; diameter and circumference; Roman numerals; graphs, graphics, maps, tables; equations; standard and metric measures including temperature; using calculator and computer.

Grade 6—Instructional focus is on: using the four basic operations on multiple-digit numbers, fractions, decimals; using standard and metric measures for temperature and liquids; volume; the mean; properties of triangles, squares, and rectangles; equations; ratio and proportion; percent; estimating and rounding; writing numbers up to twelve digits; problem solving; Roman numerals; tables, graphs, maps, charts; using calculator and computer.

ADVANCED ARITHMETIC A—Instructional focus is on: manipulating real numbers; understanding ratio and proportion formulas; gaining facility in converting metric and standard measures; writing and solving equations and inequalities; solving word and number problems; percents and percentages; understanding the distributive principle; factoring; decimals; arithmetic operations in other bases than ten; number line; graphs, maps, tables; using calculator and computer.

ADVANCED ARITHMETIC B—Instructional focus is on: manipulating real numbers; sets; ratio and proportion formulas; equations and inequalities; consumer arithmetic; operations with integral exponents; prime factoring; solving simple equations; using number lines; estimating; beginning concepts of plane geometry; tables, graphs, maps; standard and metric measures; problem solving; using calculators and computers.

PRE-ALGEBRA—Instructional focus is on: manipulation of real numbers; properties of number systems; operations with decimals; factoring; integers; rational numbers; reading, writing and solving equations and inequalities; translation of word problems to number sentences; standard and metric measures; coordinate geometry; using calculators and computers.

ALGEBRA I—Instructional focus is on: use of the variable in algebra; evaluating and simplifying algebraic expressions; equation-solving techniques; translating verbal statements to algebra; linear equations and their graphs; systems of graphs, equations, and solutions; absolute value and inequalities; polynomials and factoring; quadratic equations; quadratic formula; problem solving; using calculators and computers.

ALGEBRA II—Instructional focus is on: recognizing and using axioms; manipulating equations; understanding systems of equations and inequalities; using theorems and indirect proofs; analyzing and solving problems; graphing equalities and inequalities; solving first-degree and quadratic functions; computing accurately; identifying factoring forms; manipulating radical expressions; understanding and using formulas, complex numbers, log tables, estimation; solving polynomials; using computers and calculators.

GEOMETRY—Instructional focus is on: using a straight edge, compass, protractor; writing and reading formal indirect and analytical proofs; induction and deduction; postulates, theorems and proofs; solving geometric problems with basic algebra; using tables to solve trigonometric problems; lines, angles, triangles, polygons, quadrilaterals, circles, arcs, sectors, segments, prisms, pyramids; planes of solids; lateral areas; total areas; volumes and capacities of solids; graphing; using calculators and computers.

CONSUMER MATHEMATICS—Instructional focus is on: transforming verbal sentences to mathematical sentences; manipulating numbers skillfully; handling calculators and computers efficiently; managing aspects of practical math including: budgets, mortgages, checking and savings accounts, simple and compound interest, discounts, credit; insurance; taxes; understanding the market including: stocks, bonds, put, call, long, short, commodities; reading stock market pages with understanding.

MATH ANALYSIS—Instructional focus is on: the reinforcing of manipulative skills; using proofs; using and understanding the behavior, application and properties of circular, trigonometric and logarithmic functions; using analytic geometry; vectors; real and rational exponents; laws of sines and cosines; using calculators and computers.

CALCULUS A (Differential—Instructional focus is on: the calculus related to the functions and their derivatives; applying the derivatives; reinforcing manipulative skills; developing and constructing proofs; direct and indirect proofs; proofs by induction; properties, behavior and application of circular, trigonometric, logarithmic, exponential and polynomial functions; analytical geometry; conic sections and vectors; using computers and calculators.

CALCULUS B (INTEGRAL)—Instructional focus is on: the functions of a single variable; an infinite series; differential equations; theoretical tools of calculus; derivatives; vectors and parametric equations; polar coordinates; transcendental functions; applying integral calculus; theorems and derivations; applications to engineering, economics, physics; computer and calculator use.

Some school systems offer math courses under a variety of names. In addition to, or instead of the above, courses such as the following may be found:

- Remedial Arithmetic—Grades 7–9, review of all arithmetic processes.
- Trigonometry—Grades 10–12, similar to Math Analysis above.
- Solid Geometry—Grades 11–12, combining aspects of what is described in Geometry and Math Analysis above.
- Advanced Calculus

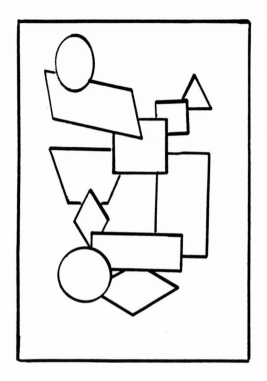

MATHEMATICS IN THE CLASSROOM

Grade K

Coming into the grade a student should:

- Be familiar with the concepts and names of colors, shapes, direction including up, down, in, out, here, there;
- Be able to recognize some numbers.

In the grade students are taught to:

- Use and compare long, short, big, small, tall, equal, not equal, fast, slow, left, right, top, bottom, above, below;
- Name geometric figures including: triangle, rectangle, circle, square; recognize likenesses and differences of shapes;
- Read and write numbers through 10; apply facts of number order (sequence) and counting through 10; compare value of numbers through 10; count from 1 to 20;
- Understand use of clocks and calendars;
- Use the ordinal terms of "first" through "fifth";

- Match groups, objects and numbers, 0 through 10;
- Recognize pennies, nickles, dimes and their worth;
- Use a computer and a calculator.

Grade 1

Coming into the grade a student should be able to:

- Recognize, name and locate colors, shapes, directions, sizes;
- Correctly use some, more, less, relative to quantity;
- Recognize, sequence and manipulate numbers from 0 to 5;
- Understand the concept of none and match it to 0;
- Recognize and understand the number concepts of pennies, nickles and dimes;
- Do simple things with a calculator and a computer keyboard.

In the grade students are taught to:

- Recognize, write and properly sequence numbers from 0 to 50;
- Use and understand mathematical symbols including: (>) more, (<) less, (+) add, (−) subtract, (=) equals, (c) cents, ($) dollars;
- Memorize addition and subtraction facts up to number 10;
- Add three single-digit numbers with sums up to 10;
- Add and subtract two-digit numbers with no regrouping (carrying) up to sums of 20;
- Count by ones, fives, tens up to 100;
- Break groups into equal parts and recognize inequalities;
- Measure length using standard and metric rulers;
- Tell time to the hour and half hour; read a digital watch;
- Develop understanding of value of "half"; understand concepts of half, third, fourth;
- Recognize value of pennies, nickles, dimes, quarters;
- Find day and date on a calendar;
- Understand commutative property of addition (2 + 3 yields the same quantity as 3 + 2);
- Use rebus for problem solving;
- Understand place value of units and tens;
- Solve word and number problems;
- Use with understanding ordinal terms from first to tenth;
- Use liquid measure in standard and metric (liter, half-liter);
- Understand and use computer terms; use a calculator.

Grade 2

Coming into the grade a student should be able to:

- Read, write and order numbers through 50;
- Use ordinals from first through tenth;
- Understand the place value of ones and tens;
- Add 2 double-digit/3 single-digit numbers with sums to 20
- Demonstrate immediate recall of number facts of addition and subtraction through 10;
- Solve addition and subtraction problems of two-digit numbers without carrying;
- Recognize and name circles, squares, triangles, rectangles;
- Use a computer keyboard and a calculator.

In the grade students are taught to:

- Write, order and compare numbers up to 999;
- Add up to 3 three-digit numbers with and without carrying;
- Subtract three-digit numbers with and without carrying;
- Regroup numbers up to 99 into tens and ones;
- Count by twos, threes, and fives up to thirty;
- Use repeated addition and arrays of twos, threes and fives to develop multiplication readiness;
- Measure time in minutes, hours, days, weeks, months, years; tell time to nearest quarter hour;

In the grade students are taught to:

- Measure length and volume in standard and metric terms;
- Interpret bar, picture, and line graphs, and maps;
- Use number line to find sums and differences to 20;
- Find a missing addend and minuend; solve rebus examples;
- Read and solve word and number problems involving addition and subtraction;
- Estimate to nearest tenth;
- Demonstrate immediate recall of number facts of all numbers through 12 in both addition and subtraction;
- Understand balancing equations $(5 + 4 = 8 +)$;
- Recognize symmetry among shapes and name shapes;
- Know value of all coins up to and including a dollar;
- Understand place value of units, tens and hundreds;
- Name and order days of the week and months of the year;

- Understand and use half, third, fourth;
- Recognize the commutative property in addition $(4 + 3 = 3 + 4)$;
- Understand and use symbols including $(<)$, $(>)$, $(+)$, $(-)$, $(\times)$, $(\div)$, $(\$)$, (c);
- Understand identity element in addition (0).

Grade 3

Coming into the grade a student should be able to:

- Read, write and order numbers through 100;
- Add and subtract up to three-digit numbers with carrying;
- Provide immediate response on addition and subtraction number facts through number 12; count by twos, threes, fives to 30;
- Tell time to nearest half hour;
- Use standard and metric scales for measuring;
- Solve word problems involving addition and subtraction;
- Use coins in calculations up to $1.00;
- Name geometric forms; use a number line to compute;
- Understand and use thirds, fourths, halves;
- Use a computer and calculator.

In the grade students are taught to:

- Add up to 3 three-digit numbers and 2 four-digit numbers with carrying; subtract 1-, 2-, 3- and 4-digit numbers from a 4-digit number with carrying (exchange);
- Multiply, using both horizontal and vertical form, of up to a 2-digit number by a 1-digit number with carrying;

In the grade students are taught to:

- Divide a two-digit number by a one-digit number, with a remainder;
- Write fractions and mixed numbers to describe groups;
- Develop decimal concepts; estimate to nearest tenth;
- Compute and make change to $10.00;
- Understand and use standard and metric measures (inches, feet, yards, miles, centimeters, meters, half-pint, pint, quart, gallon, gram, kilogram, liter;
- Solve word and number problems and use rebus;
- Read and interpret line graphs, bar graphs, pictographs and maps;
- Identify plane and solid geometric figures including circles, squares, triangles, rectangles, cubes, cones, spheres;

- Compare, order, contrast cardinal numbers to 999; ordinals to one hundredth;
- Transpose algorithms (examples) from horizontal to vertical form and vise versa;
- Use measuring devices appropriately;
- Demonstrate immediate recall of number facts in addition, subtraction, multiplication and division through the twelves;
- Understand properties of 0 and 1 as identity elements;
- Use commutative and associative property in addition and multiplication;
- Compute equations and inequalities; use number line.

Grade 4

Coming into the grade a student should be able to:

- Read, write, order and compare numbers up to 999; ordinals;
- Add combinations of numbers up to three 3-digit numbers; subtract up to 3-digit numbers; multiply any 3-digit number by a 1-digit number; divide a 2-digit number by a 1-digit number;
- Read and write fractions; identify geometric shapes;
- Create arrays to show multiplication and division facts;
- Convert standard to metric measures and vice versa;
- Tell time to nearest quarter hour;
- Measure length to nearest inch;
- Write monetary values in numbers to $10.00;
- Check all operations.

In the grade students are taught to:

- Add up to 5-digit numbers using money notation when appropriate;
- Subtract up to 4-digit numbers using money when appropriate;
- Multiply by a 2-digit number; divide by a 2-digit number;
- Round money to nearest dollar, and add, subtract, multiply, divide;
- Determine needed processes for solving problems, and estimate results before seeking solutions;
- Convert standard to metric measures and back; use centimeter, meter, kilometer, centigram, gram, liter, milliliter, inch, foot, mile, ounce, pound, ton, cups, pints, quarts, gallons;
- Write hours and minutes; use calendar;
- Add and subtract fractional mixed numbers with like denominators; find fractional part of whole numbers; convert to decimal from

mixed number; add and subtract decimals up to hundredths; write decimals in columns;

- Understand area, volume, angles, triangles, circles, pentagons, quadrilaterals, points, lines, perimeter, radius, diameter, cube, sphere, pyramid, cone, cylinder;
- Write standard form for numbers up to millions; horizontal and vertical forms for examples; words for numbers and numbers for all number-words; write decimals, fractions, Roman numerals; ordinals;
- Provide immediate response for all number facts of addition, subtraction, multiplication, and division up through twelves;
- Interpret and construct line and bar graphs, maps, tables, charts;
- Estimate; round to nearest tenth; check answer using inverse;
- Solve arithmetic equations and inequalities; use number line;
- Use commutative, associative, distributive principles;
- Use a computer and calculator.

Grade 5

Coming into the grade a student should be able to:

- Read and write all numbers in standard numerical and word form through millions;
- Add and subtract four-digit numbers with carrying; multiply and divide by a one-digit number with carrying and remainders;
- Manipulate and compute fractions with like denominators; decimals up to hundredths; respond to all number facts;
- Calculate money; interpret tables, graphs, maps.

In the grade students are taught to:

- Add and subtract numbers up to 6 digits with carrying;
- Multiply and divide by a 2-digit number using zero;
- Add, subtract and multiply like and unlike fractions; find least common denominator; find greatest common factor; write equivalent fractions; reduce to simplest form; change to decimals and reconvert; add, subtract and multiply decimals; change decimals and fractions to percents;
- Solve problems using all basic operations;
- Solve arithmetic equations and inequalities; find average (mean);
- Measure to nearest half inch and centimeter; use tables of measures; use Fahrenheit and Celsius scales for temperature;
- Compute money using all basic operations;

- Identify linear and solid forms; parallels, perpendiculars, horizontals, verticals; diameter and circumference of circles; perimeter and area of rectangles and triangles;
- Compute time using knowledge of seconds in minute, minutes in hour, hours in day, days in month, months in year, years in decade and century; compute time using conversion; use calendar; use graphs, maps, charts, tables;
- Estimate, round and check all answers;
- Write, order and compare numbers through billions;
- Provide immediate response on number facts through twelves;
- Understand place value; read and write Roman numerals;
- Use a computer and calculator.

Grade 6

Coming into the grade a student should be able to:

- Read and write all numbers in numerical and word form;
- Round numbers up to 10,000 to nearest tenth or hundredth;
- Add and subtract multiple-digit numbers with carrying;
- Multiply and divide by 2-digit numbers with carrying;
- Add, subtract and multiply fractions and mixed numbers with unlike denominators; reduce fractions;
- Add, subtract, multiply decimals to hundredths;
- Change decimals and fractions to percents;
- Use standard and metric units of measurement;
- Find perimeter and area of rectangle; circumference and diameter of circle;
- Demonstrate immediate recall of number facts.

In the grade students are taught to:

- Write, order and compare values of any rational, fractional, or decimal numbers in numerical and verbal form;
- Add, subtract, multiply, and divide multiple-digit numbers;
- Read and solve problems needing estimation and computation and involving whole numbers, decimals, fractions, time, money, distance, percents, averages, graphs;
- Measure and compute in standard and metric scales;
- Divide fractions and decimals; use inversion; practice addition, subtraction and multiplication of fractions and decimals; convert decimals to fractions—fractions to decimals—both to percent;

- Compute ratio and proportion; solve equations and inequalities;
- Memorize formulas for finding answers to problems involving area, distance, interest, circumference and others;
- Construct and interpret scale drawings, graphs, maps;
- Factor whole numbers into primes; greatest common factor;
- Identify all geometric shapes;
- Understand use of exponents of numbers;
- Understand and use place value; use identity elements 0 and 1;
- Understand and use number lines;
- Identify and write Roman numerals;
- Review arrays and number facts;
- Use commutative, associative and distributive principles;
- Use computer and calculator.

Advanced Arithmetic A (Grades 7–9)

Coming into the class a student should demonstrate:

- Ability to compute whole numbers, decimals, fractions, using all four computation skills and demonstrating immediate recall of number facts through twelves;
- Understanding the identity elements of 0 and 1;
- Facility using and computing standard and metric measures;
- Ability to read and write Roman numerals; standard numerals through billions;
- Ability to compute money, time, measurements;
- Ability to use computer and calculator.

In the class students are taught to:

- Perform basic operations on whole numbers, fractions and decimals;
- Apply simple formulas for solving problems involving ratio, proportion, area, perimeter, volume;
- Solve problems involving percentages, including interest, discount, increase, decrease, commissions;
- Memorize and use formulas for standard-metric conversions;
- Find greatest common factor; least common multiple;
- Solve arithmetic equations; find square root; use exponents;
- Memorize and use the Pythagorean theorem;
- Understand consumer arithmetic including: discount, credit, interest, loans, mortgages, writing checks, budgeting;
- Understand the set of rational numbers;

- Use of > for greater than and < for less than and letters as substitutes for numbers to describe processes; (R = rational numbers; > = greater than; R > 0 = rational number greater than 0)
- Solve problems using estimation; use number lines;
- Understand place value and other base systems;
- Use the commutative, associative and distributive principles;
- Use a computer and calculator.

Advanced Arithmetic B (Grades 8–10)

Coming into the class a student should demonstrate:

- Ability to perform basic operations on all whole numbers, fractions, decimals; ability to solve problems and equations;
- Immediate recall of number facts;
- Ability to read and understand set notation;
- Ability to read, understand and solve arithmetic word problems;
- Ability to understand, compute and convert metric and standard;
- Ability to convert fractions, decimals and percents;
- Dexterity in use of computer and calculator.

In the class students are taught to:

- Manipulate real numbers (denoted R), integers (denoted J) and sets of rationals;
- Find square roots using algorisms and tables;
- Write and solve equations and inequalities; find missing terms;

In the class students are taught to:

- Compute with complex fractions and decimals;
- Operate with integral exponents; use exponents with multiplication and division;
- Manipulate proportions; operate and simplify ratios on the set of natural numbers and the set of real numbers;
- Factor composite numbers; identify prime numbers;
- Use formulas to solve problems;
- Perform simple operations on right triangles;
- Graph using coordinates; read maps;
- Compute examples of elementary probability;
- Review consumer arithmetic from Advanced Arithmetic A;
- Compute measurement problems and money problems;
- Construct and use number lines;

- Compute in other base systems; review place value;
- Take notes and keep a notebook for reference;
- Use a computer and calculator.

Pre-Algebra

(Designed for students who need more and better mastery of arithmetic skills before attempting algebra.)

Coming into the class a student should demonstrate:

- Immediate response on all number facts;
- Ability to add, subtract, multiply, divide;
- Ability to use a calculator.

In the class students will:

- Review operations on the set of rational (whole) numbers;
- Review positive and negative numbers and their interaction;
- Review properties of fractions and decimals and operations on them; review ratio, proportion and percentage; convert decimals, fractions and percents; problems of interest, discount, percent of increase and decrease, markup, commission;
- Review geometric problems and solutions including parallels, perpendiculars, similar and congruent polygons, area and volume of planes and solids and the appropriate formulas;
- Review simple statistics and probability; square numbers and find square roots; use calculators and computers.
- Write and solve linear equations and linear inequalities; graph solutions; construct and use number lines;
- Use the processes of estimating and rounding;
- Translate verbal problems to number statements and reverse.

Algebra I

Coming into the class a student should demonstrate ability to:

- Perform basic operations on whole numbers, fractions, decimals and percents;
- Simplify complex fractions; convert fractions to decimals and percents; compute ratio and proportion;
- Estimate and round numbers; understand use of exponents;
- Understand factors, factoring, primes, multiples;
- Demonstrate recall of basic formulas and of number facts.

In the class students are taught to:

- Understand the basic language of algebra: real numbers, number lines, sets, variables, expressions;
- Understand the properties of real numbers and the system created by them;
- Understand the fundamental operations of the rational and irrational numbers; understand absolute value of a number;
- Solve equalities and inequalities with one variable;
- Use axioms of equality and inequality in writing proofs;
- Perform operations with polynomials; understand laws of exponents; find products of monomials and polynomials, special products and prime factors of polynomials;
- Compute algebraic fractions; simplify complex fractions; solve ratio and proportion problems; understand percent and its algebraic applications;
- Solve quadratic equations by factoring; solve fractional equations with constant denominators; with polynomials in denominators;
- Graph linear equalities and inequalities; functions; relation; slope; y-intercept; direct variation;
- Solve 2-by-2 systems of linear equations; use graphing and algebraic techniques;
- Solve problems of motion, investment, mixture, coins, geometry, percent, levers, fractions;
- Create and evaluate formulas;
- Keep a useable notebook; use a calculator and a computer.

$$x^2 + (2x - y) \times 4y = a^2$$

Algebra II

Coming into the class a student should demonstrate ability to:

- Evaluate algebraic expressions using rational numbers;
- Create and evaluate formulas;
- Add, subtract, multiply and divide signed numbers;
- Evaluate expressions using signed numbers;
- Calculate numbers in parenthesis;

- Process polynomials; monomials; simplify;
- Solve linear equalities and inequalities with one variable; 2-by-2 system with two variables; second-degree equations with one variable by factoring;
- Solve fractional equations with numerical denominators.

In the class students are taught to:

- Understand and use the field postulates and real numbers system; other systems and their properties;
- Understand axioms of the field and their use in proofs;
- Manipulate polynomials including factoring and finding prime factors; handle problems and solutions of absolute value;
- Understand functions and relations: domain, range, graphing;
- Understand consistent and inconsistent linear systems and solutions by 3-by-3 linear systems;
- Solve equations and inequalities using factoring and the real number line; express solutions as open and closed intervals or half-open intervals; simplify rational expressions;
- Work with roots; radicals; simplify irrational numbers;
- Solve quadratic equations; understand nature of the roots using the discriminant; understand systems of quadratics;
- Understand properties of the complex number system;
- Solve irrational equations and exponential equations;
- Work with exponential and logarithmic functions, significant digits, scientific notation, common logarithms;
- Use binomial theorem; use expansion patterns and properties;
- Use synthetic substitution; synthetic division;
- Use axioms and theorems to prove conditionals; use indirect proofs;
- Analyze problems; use computers and calculators.

Geometry

Coming into the class a student should demonstrate ability to:

- Evaluate algebraic expressions using the rational numbers;
- Perform basic operations on signed numbers;
- Manipulate numbers in parenthesis;
- Perform basic operations on, and simplify, polynomials and algebraic fractions;
- Solve linear equalities and inequalities; use factoring;

- Solve fractional equations with numerical denominators, with variables in denominator and with decimals;
- Use compass, protractor and straight edge;
- Find area, perimeter, volume, diameter, radius, angle, congruency.

In the class students are taught to:

- Understand elements of geometry; use the language of sets;
- Understand induction (method of discovery); deduction (method of proof); nature of proof; impossibility of defining all terms or proving all statements; work within the principles of logic;
- Use initial postulates and theorems; use mathematical systems;
- Understand angles and their measure; determine angle relationships and employ formal proofs;
- Discover characteristics of parallel lines, polygons, planes;
- Prove congruency of triangles, of corresponding parts;
- Define and prove similarity; prove similar polygons, triangles;
- Understand the Pythagorean theorem and its applications;
- Construct and compute measurements of circles, triangles, arcs, chords, angles, segments, quadrilaterals, polygons;
- Graph ordered pairs, lines; find and use distances;
- Find the areas of polygons and circles; do proofs using coordinates;
- Find the areas, volume and capacity of solids; prisms, pyramids, cylinders;
- Understand and use correct techniques of writing formal proofs, indirect proofs, analytic proofs;
- Use basic algebra and trigonometric tables to solve geometric problems; use computers and calculators.

Consumer Mathematics (Generally a one-semester course)

Coming into the class a student should demonstrate ability to:

- Calculate with the four basic operations on whole numbers, fractions, decimals and percents;
- Convert fractions to decimals and percents and reverse;
- Round off and estimate;
- Use a computer and a calculator.

In the class students are taught to:

- Price merchandise including: trade discount, trade price, cash discount, successive discounts, markup, percent of markup, percent of markdown;

- Compute interest including: formulas, simple interest yearly and monthly, daily interest, savings and checking account interest, compound interest, using interest tables;
- Understand costs of borrowing money including: time loan, demand loan, mortgages, balloon payments, discounting a note, installment buying, charge accounts, automobile loans;
- Understand cost and coverage of insurance including: life insurance, term insurance, health insurance, automobile insurance;
- Understand and compute taxes including: real estate tax, sales tax, municipal tax, county tax, state tax, federal tax, luxury tax, licenses, other taxes;
- Write checks and balance checkbooks;
- Understand stocks, bonds and commodities trading;
- Create and use budgets;
- Solve problems involving consumer situations;
- Use calculators and computers.

Math Analysis

Coming into the class a student should demonstrate ability to:

- Factor on the real numbers;
- Perform all basic operations on fractions; reduce fractions;
- Simplify irrational numbers; understand exponents;
- Perform operations on complex numbers;
- Use logarithms, binomial expansion, synthetic substitution, synthetic division, determinants including: consistent, inconsistent, indeterminant;

Coming into the class a student should demonstrate ability to:

- Solve equations including: linear, 2-by-2 and 3-by-3 linear systems, fractional quadratic, systems of quadratics, irrational, logarithmic, exponential;
- Use the trigonometry of the right triangle;
- Solve verbal problems involving the above.

In the class students are taught to:

- Understand and use real and complex numbers and order relations;
- Use mathematical induction; logic; solve inequalities;

- Use and understand functions and mappings; inverse functions; composition of functions; wrapping function;
- Understand distance and circles; trigonometric functions; sine and cosine; graphs of sine and cosine; tangent and cotangent;
- Understand amplitude and period; phase shift;
- Describe and compute angles and rotation; radian measure;
- Use reduction formulas;
- Compute using sum and difference identities; double- and half-angle identities; sum and product forms;
- Use inverse circular functions; inverses and determinants;
- Solve trigonometric equations and inequalities;
- Understand complex numbers in polar form; polar coordinates;
- Approximate zeros of a polynomial; polynomial functions;
- Compute with rational exponents; real exponents;
- Understand and use logarithmic function; exponential function;
- Understand vectors including: operations, perpendicular vectors, norm of a vector, linear combinations of vectors, perpendicular and parallel components of vectors; resolution of vectors; vector equation of lines in a plane;
- Understand dot product (inner); cross product;
- Compute problems involving ellipse, parabola, hyperbola, circle; investigate rotations of conics;
- Construct matrices; solve systems equations with matrices;
- Use field postulates and proofs;
- Work with theorems including: De Moivres, remainder and factor, rational root.

Calculus A (Differential)

Coming into the class a student should demonstrate ability to:

- Perform operations on reduction of fractions; on complex numbers; use trigonometry of the right angle;
- Handle exponents on integral, rational and irrational numbers;
- Factor on the real numbers; handle logarithms; binomial expansions; synthetic substitutions;
- Understand determinants including: consistent, inconsistent, indeterminant; third-order determinants by minor;
- Simplify irrational numbers; solve equations including: linear, 2-by-2

and 2-by-3 linear systems, fractional, quadratics, systems of quadratics, irrational, logarithmic, exponential.

Information and skills to be presented in the class include:

- Functions including: wrapping, sine and cosine, tangent and cosine functions, trigonometric and circular, trigonometric and triangles, inverse circular, inverse trigonometric, polynomial, rational, exponential, the function log u;
- Derivatives including: derivatives of functions, of implicit relation, chain rule, sign of first derivative, significance of sign of second derivative, derivative of ln x; transcendental functions and their derivatives;
- Values of sine x and cosine x; graphs of sine and cosine;
- Amplitude and period; phase shift;
- Angles and rotation; angles measured in radians;
- Identities; sum and difference identities for sine and tangent; double- and half-angle identities; sum and product identities;
- Law of sines; law of cosines; reduction formulas;
- Equations and inequalities involving trigonometric functions;
- Complex numbers in polar form; polar coordinates; roots and powers; De Moivres theorem; synthetic substitution;
- Remainder and factor theorems;
- Locating real zeros; rational zeros; number of zeros of a polynomial function; properties of limits;
- Formulas for differentials repeated in notation of differentials; differentials dx and dy; related rates;
- Curve sketches and plots; second-degree curves;
- Maxima and minima theory; maxima and minima problems;
- Rolle's theorem; mean-value theorem;
- The natural logarithm; tangents and normals;
- Invariants and the discriminant.

Calculus B (Advanced)

Coming into the class a student should show understanding of:

- Real and complex numbers; field postulates and proof; order relations; graphs; solutions of inequalities; mathematical induction; absolute value; functions and mappings;
- Wrapping function; sine and cosine function; amplitude and period; phase shift; tangent and cotangent; angles and rotation; identities;

radian; trigonometric functions; sum and difference identities; double- and half-angle identities; sum and product forms; functions and inverses; reduction formulas;

- Laws of sines and cosines; trigonometric equations and inequalities; inverse of circular functions; complex numbers in polar form; polar coordinates; De Moivres theorem;
- Polynomial functions; synthetic division and substitution;
- Remainder, factor and rational root theorems;
- Zeros and approximating zeros of a polynomial; rational and real exponents; inverses; vectors; vector operations.

Information and skills to be presented in the class:

- Review of functions and derivatives; slopes of straight lines and curves; equations of straight lines; velocity and rates; properties of limits;
- Integration: indefinite integral and applications; differentiation and integration of sines and cosines; area under a curve; computation of areas as limits; areas by calculus; definite integral and fundamental theorem on integral calculus; trapezoidal rule for approximating an integral; notation; area between 2 curves; distance; volumes; length of plane curve; area of a surface of revolution; average value of function;
- Applications of integration to physics: moments and center of gravity; theorems of Pappus; moments of inertia; radius of gyration; parallel axis theorem; hydrostatic pressure; work;
- Review of transcendental functions: trigonometric, inverse trigonometric, natural logarithm, derivative of ln x; exponential function; function of au; differential equations;
- Methods of integration: formulas; powers of trigonometric functions; integrals involving $a2 - u2$; integrals involving $ax2 + bx + c$; integration by partial fractions; rational functions of sine x and cosine x; improper integrals;
- Vectors and parametric equations in kinematics, in analytic geometry; components of unit vectors i and j; differentiation of vectors; tangential vectors; curvature and normal vectors; vector velocity and acceleration; polar coordinates.

Chapter 11

MUSIC IN THE CLASSROOM

OVERVIEW

Music is taught as a part of other subject areas and as a special subject throughout the grades. All students are given the opportunity to learn to read music and to play instruments. Not all choose to do so. All students participate in singing. Music electives are usually offered in the secondary grades.

Grade K—Opportunities are provided for students to: identify tempo and duration; match tones in singing; identify sounds of rhythm instruments; respond to music with mood, feeling and body movement; develop primary listening skills; identify keyboard notes; sing the national anthem.

Grade 1—Students learn to: accompany singing with rhythm instruments; sing rounds; use basic music symbols; read simple melodies using numbers and then notes; practice rhythm skills; listen with purpose to a variety of music records and recitals; sing a variety of patriotic and other songs.

Grade 2—Students are helped to: develop vocal skills; develop better listening skills; identify notes in a scale; recognize timbre of instruments; identify form, contrast and repetition in music; choose whether to play instrument; select instrument; listen to music for enjoyment; move to music.

Grade 3—Students refine ability to: identify pitch and rhythm patterns; recognize major scales and tone colors; play instruments and read music; read notes on a musical staff; recognize note value; enhance listening skills and music appreciation; sing two-part songs; sing in class choruses.

Grade 4—Students refine ability to: identify pitch and rhythm patterns; recognize major scales and tone colors; play instruments and read music; read notes on a musical staff; recognize note value; enhance listening skills and music appreciation; sing two-part songs; sing in class choruses.

Grade 5 — Instructional focus is on: syncopation and various dance rhythms; homophony and polyphony; music of ballet, opera, concerto, symphony; two-part singing; singing for fun; moving to music; reading music on staff for rhythm and simple singing; performing in orchestra or band or chorus.

Grade 6 — Instructional focus is on: discriminating between sounds of major and minor scales; singing major and harmonic minor scales from written music with and without accompaniment; listening to music for appreciation; moving to music; singing for fun; performing in orchestra, band or chorus.

Most school systems require some music courses in secondary grades, but for the most part, music instruction is an elective. The courses described below are typical of offerings in junior and senior high school grades and are not specific to any particular grade.

GENERAL MUSIC STUDY — Instructional focus is on: properties of sound and music including pitch, duration, intensity, timbre; presentation and analysis of musicals, classical music, jazz, rock and electronic sound; singing in chorus; notation and music theory; music history and appreciation.

CHORUS — Instructional focus is on: theory and notation; emphasis on two- and three-part singing; identification of individual voice ranges; singing with and without accompaniment; singing for enjoyment; singing for audiences.

BAND — Instructional focus is on: providing students with the opportunity to play chosen instruments along with other students; following a conductor; preparing for concerts, athletic events and parades; developing marching skills; reading music for band instruments.

CONCERT CHOIR — Instructional focus is on: studying and performing choral literature from all periods; improving music reading skills; following a conductor; listening to performances; honing singing skills.

ORCHESTRA — Instructional focus is on: study and performance of orchestral literature of present as well as previous periods; characteristics of instruments; styles of composition and performance; improving reading and playing skills.

ENSEMBLE — Instructional focus is on: chamber music groups composed of families of instruments (strings, woodwinds, . . .); opportunity to play and perform in small ensembles.

MUSIC IN THE CLASSROOM

Grade K

Coming into the grade a student should be able to:

- Hear, listen, follow simple directions;
- Produce vocal sounds; move to music.

In the grade students are taught to:

- Use all rhythm instruments; respond to rhythm patterns;
- Sing short one- and two-part melodies alone and with the group;
- Remember words and music of simple songs;
- Identify natural and man-made sounds.

Grade 1

Coming into the grade a student should be able to:

- Move, clap and play rhythm instruments to a beat;
- Sing short melodies including simple two-part songs;
- Play and move to music.

In the grade students are taught to:

- Recognize changes in tempo and duration of musical sounds;
- Identify simple chords; identify sound sources;
- Improve rhythm instrument skills; combine sound sources;
- Sing alone and with a group; sing for fun;
- Listen to records and tapes and appreciate performances.

Grade 2

Coming into the grade a student should be able to:

- Recognize tempo and duration changes, chords, sound sources;
- Produce movement and sound to a beat;
- Sing words and music of many songs.

In the grade students are taught to:

- Associate pitch with symbols (notation) and instruments;
- Sustain a melodic line against a harmonic accompaniment;
- Illustrate with hand motion the direction of the melody;
- Sing rounds; accompany singing with rhythm instruments;

- Learn to sing traditional and modern songs.

Grade 3

Coming into the grade a student should be able to:

- Sing traditional and modern songs and rounds;
- Illustrate with hand motions the direction of a melody;
- Recognize musical symbols (notes, staff).

In the grade students are taught to:

- Play a simple instrument (recorder, autoharp, other);
- Care for an instrument properly; tuning;
- Read and understand musical notation including note value, key, stop and repeat symbols;
- Produce music from interpreting simple notation;
- Sing in large and small groups and listen to music.

Grade 4

Coming into the grade a student should be able to:

- Play simple tunes on an instrument; read notation;
- Phrase music when singing;
- Tune and care for an instrument.

In the grade students are taught to:

- Read and respond to all note values, rest values, slurs;
- Understand key signatures; copy notation;
- Understand and illustrate chords up to octaves;
- Understand and respond to specialized musical vocabulary such as crescendo, decrescendo, accellerando;
- Learn new songs and sing for pleasure and performance;
- Become familiar with works of great musicians.

Grade 5

Coming into the grade a student should be able to:

- Read and write musical notation;
- Play an instrument and/or sing in harmony;
- Identify selected works of great musicians and composers.

In the grade students are taught to:

- Understand how music is used to express mood, emotions, ideas; recognize elements of expressive composition;
- Recognize and respond to monophonic (single melody), homophonic (melody with chords) and polyphonic music;
- Listen appreciatively to selected musical performances;
- Learn new songs and sing for pleasure and performance;
- Continue to improve instrumental skills;
- Expand knowledge and appreciation of musical compositions.

Grade 6

Coming into the grade a student should be able to:

- Recognize and respond to rhythm sets, melodies and intervals using hand signals; textures in harmony, form; and dynamic markings in notation;
- Identify and appreciate musical selections.

In the grade students are taught to:

- Examine the history and development of music; identify great composers and performers;
- Increase skills of reading and performing music (vocal and instrumental) in major and minor keys;
- Sing rounds, canons, popular and traditional songs;
- Demonstrate knowledge of rhythm, movement and art of music.

Grades 7–8

Coming into the grades a student should be able to:

- Read notation and perform vocally and/or instrumentally;
- Recognize and appreciate different musical forms;
- Respond to mood, emotion and color in music.

In the grades students are taught to:

- Understand and appreciate the history of American music; world music; musical theatre; jazz;
- Recognize and appreciate differences in musical styles;
- Understand the development of musical instruments and the modern-day orchestra, band, ensemble;
- Identify timbre of instruments;

- Relate music to drama and dance;
- Improve vocal techniques and singing skills.

Grades 9–12: Elective—Concert Choir

Coming into the class a student should demonstrate:

- Skills and abilities acquired in previous grades with reference to singing and reading music.

In the class students are taught to:

- Use maturing voices in performance of choral literature;
- Recognize various forms of choral music;
- Critically evaluate a performance; sing on key with and without accompaniment;
- Sing in other languages; breathe correctly.

Grades 9–12: Elective—Marching Band

Coming into the class a student should demonstrate ability to:

- Play an instrument; read notation;
- Respond appropriately to a conductor.

In the class students are taught to:

- March and respond to marching signals while playing; move in formations;

- Play various school songs and pop tunes with pride and spirit;
- Develop a sense of responsibility to and for the group.

Grades 9–12: Elective—Orchestra and/or Chamber Groups

Coming into the class a student should demonstrate ability to:

- Play an instrument; read notation;
- Enjoy music.

In the class students are taught to:

- Follow a conductor and concentrate on individual part;
- Play accurately and with artistry; select appropriate music;
- Understand qualities of major and minor compositions;
- Interpret music and perform for audiences.

Chapter 12

PHYSICAL EDUCATION IN THE CLASSROOM

OVERVIEW

Most states require that students participate in physical education classes during every school year. Activities offered are meant to take advantage of natural physical development and the increased control of motor skills students achieve as they mature. Life skills and game rules are taught. Sportsmanship and cooperation are stressed. Where appropriate, offerings are individualized. Ability levels based on past successes are taken into account in working toward new levels of achievement. Safety is taught and emphasized.

Grade K—Students participate in: gross motor skill exercises; floor exercises which use the whole body to best advantage; simple climbing skills; cardiovascular strengthening; basic ball skills; tumbling and mat skills; coordination drills, games.

Grade 1—Students are instructed in: safety skills; balancing; team games; listening skills; climbing; hurdling; tunneling; falling; left-right discrimination; basic gross motor skills; ball skills; fitness skills; long and short jump rope skills; exercises for coordination; moving to music.

Grade 2—Students are instructed in: proper use of indoor and outdoor equipment; safety; body capability and image; left-right discrimination; gross motor skills; ball skills; mat and fitness, balance and climbing skills; team games; coordination exercises; long and short jump rope skills; moving to music.

Grade 3—Students are taught and practice: ball skills and ball games; relay races; intermediate coordination exercises; mat exercises; balance activities; fitness exercises; proper use of equipment; moving to music.

Grade 4—Students are taught and practice: coordination exercises; motor skills; rhythmic skills; group and team sports; rope jumping; conditioning activities; isometric and isotonic activities; breathing; dynamic and static balance; tumbling and mat exercises; ball games; moving rhythmically to music.

Grade 5—Instructional focus is on: rules for a variety of games; interaction skills; cooperation and independence; honing skills used in: gymnastics and tumbling, balance and coordination, moving rhythmically to music, ball and rope activities; proper use and care of equipment.

Grade 6—Instructional focus is on: review of game skills taught; advanced coordination activities; more difficult balance, gymnastic and mat skills; ball and rope activities; relays and individual races; moving rhythmically to music; use and care of equipment.

Grades 7-8—Instructional focus is on: dressing appropriately for gym; selection and care of equipment appropriate to the activity; safety exercises; skill-building activities which develop endurance, suppleness, balance, strength, agility and speed; team skills and attitudes.

Grades 9-10—Instructional focus is on: development of lifetime skills including: skills, rules and equipment needs for tennis, volleyball, basketball, table tennis, badminton, softball, archery, golf, baseball, softball, soccer, bowling; developing endurance, strength, coordination and speed through aerobic exercises, breathing techniques, track and field activities, cross-country exercises; developing interactive skills through teamwork and squad work.

Grades 11-12—Instructional focus is on: body-conditioning exercises, teamwork; improvement of individual skills in all physical activities; review of rules for games, sports and lifetime skills; increasing individual proficiency levels; walking, jogging, cycling, bowling as lifetime activities along with those begun in earlier grades.

PHYSICAL EDUCATION IN THE CLASSROOM

Grade K

Coming into the grade a student should be able to:

- Listen, speak and follow directions;
- Work and play with other children;
- Recognize sameness and difference.

In the grade students are taught:

- Control of gross motor skills (walking, jumping, turning);
- Directions (forward, backward, up, down);
- Simple climbing skills (reaching, grasping, creeping);
- Basic ball skills (catching, throwing, bouncing, rolling);
- Safety in the gym and on the playground;
- Basic balance and mat skills; coordination activities;
- Exercises for strength, lower back strength and agility;
- Good sportsmanship, participation and sharing;
- Left-right discrimination; awareness of body capabilities;
- Appropriate use and care of equipment.

Grade 1

Coming into the grade a student should be able to:

- Use equipment appropriately;
- Know and practice safety rules;
- Perform some large muscle activities skillfully.

In the grade students are taught:

- The importance of physical exercise in keeping fit;
- Conditioning exercises (skipping, hopping, jogging, crawling, galloping, marching, leaping);
- Responding to directions (left, right, forward, backward, up, down, attention, at ease, etc.);
- Various balance positions; walking blocks; stilts;
- Climbing vertical, horizontal, inclined ladders;
- Hurdling, tunneling, tumbling, falling, crab walk;
- Basic ball skills (throwing, catching, rolling, bouncing);
- Basic coordination and fitness skills (calisthenics);
- Use of long and short jump ropes;

- Games and game rules stressing action and response to commands (Red Light, Statues, Duck-Duck-Goose, etc.)
- Cooperation as an individual and a team member;
- Good sportsmanship;
- Appropriate care and use of equipment.

Grade 2

Coming into the grade a student should be able to:

- Play many games according to their rules;
- Perform many gross motor skills exercises;
- Cooperate and compete as a member of a team.

In the grade students are taught:

- Safe use of indoor and outdoor equipment (ladders, ropes, swings, balls, rings, stilts, etc.);
- Leaping, skipping, hopping, marching, turning, dancing;
- Catching, throwing, bouncing while moving, standing, or sitting; jump rope skills;
- Dynamic and static balance on beam, stilts, blocks;
- Rope and pole climbing; climbing ladders; crawling;
- Calisthenic skills (jumping jacks, straddle jumps, etc.);
- Mat skills (rolls, head stand, cartwheel, back bend, bicycle);
- Basic Krauss-Weber fitness skills for increasing stamina and strengthening the body (sit-ups, push-ups, etc.);
- Team games requiring cooperation and use of equipment (dodge ball, Indian-pin relays, etc.);
- Appropriate use and care of equipment.

Grade 3

Coming into the grade a student should be able to:

- Demonstrate proficiency with gross-motor skill activities;
- Use equipment, and play learned games according to rules.

In the grade students are taught:

- Increased control of all ball skills using both hands;
- Improved skills for relay races of all kinds;
- Floor games to be played in the gym; game rules;
- Jumping jacks, squat thrusts, cross steps, broad jumps, jump rope skills with long and short ropes;

- Intermediate ball skills (overhand and underhand throws, dribbling using each hand, kicking, dribbling with feet);
- Intermediate balance skills on balance beam and pogo stick;
- Intermediate fitness activities (pull-ups, bent-arm hang, push-ups, etc.); calisthenics; dancing; intermediate mat skills (backward and shoulder rolls, head stand, tip-up, three-legged stool, cartwheel, bridges; safety rules);
- Increased ability to perform Krauss-Weber exercises.

Grade 4

Coming into the grade a student should be able to:

- Follow directions and perform tasks as requested;
- Participate and cooperate in team games;
- Perform body-conditioning exercises.

In the grade students are taught:

- Sports skills (softball, soccer, basketball, volleyball, football; game rules);
- Warm-up exercises; calisthenics and conditioning;
- Isometric and isotonic activities; breathing exercises;
- Advanced skills (jumping, ball control, mat and tumbling, dynamic and static balance, rhythmic skills and dancing);
- Safety rules and care of equipment;
- Gymnastics and aerobics; swimming (if pool is available).

Grade 5

Coming into the grade a student should be able to:

- Demonstrate knowledge of rules of selected team and individual games and sports;
- Perform Krauss-Weber skills at intermediate level or more.

In the grade students are taught:

- Relays and games relying on interaction and interdependence;
- Advanced gymnastic and tumbling activities;
- Advanced ball skills, jumping skills, tumbling skills;
- Advanced balance skills and combinations of skills;
- Appreciation and understanding of what the body can do;
- Activities which hone gross and fine motor skills;
- Adding time elements to performance of skills;

- Aerobics and rhythmic exercises; dancing routines;
- Sports skills; sports safety and regulations;
- Use and care of equipment; swimming (if pool is available).

Grade 6

Coming into the grade a student should be able to:

- Perform skills of endurance;
- Use equipment safely and adhere to rules of sports and games;
- Play with good sportsmanship.

In the grade students are taught:

- Techniques, rules and regulations of sports (basketball, baseball, softball, soccer, football, field hockey, dodge ball, volleyball, swimming—if available, etc.);
- Advanced aerobics, gymnastics, calisthenics, dancing skills; advanced coordination and balance activities;
- Track and field skills (relays, racing, jumping);
- Rules for leisure-time activities (tennis, golf, bowling);
- Techniques for honing skills of team sports;
- Fitness exercise routines; Krauss-Weber skills;
- Safety and safe use of equipment.

Grades 7–8

Coming into the grade a student should demonstrate knowledge of:

- Proper running, throwing, catching techniques;
- Ability to play in a group safely; knowledge of game rules;
- Respect for rights of others including teachers.

In the grade students are taught:

- Skills of endurance, suppleness, balance, strength, agility, speed, coordination;
- Proper preparation for strenuous activities;
- Gymnastics, aerobic and calisthenic exercises;
- Track and field skills; lifetime sports;
- Weight control; dietetics; use of equipment;
- Rhythm and dancing activities;
- Career education in sports and physical education fields;
- Participation in individual and group physical activities;
- Swimming—if pool is available.

Grades 9-10

Coming into the grade a student should demonstrate knowledge of:

- Body control in performance of physical education skills;
- Sportsmanlike participation in individual and group skills;
- Knowledge and understanding of conditioning activities;
- Some knowledge of career possibilities in the field.

In the grade students are taught the basics of:

- Tennis (backhand, forehand, serve, scoring);
- Table tennis (serving, grip, strategy, scoring);
- Softball (batting, catching, throwing, position, scoring);
- Volleyball (serving, spiking, passing, scoring);
- Basketball (passing, dribbling, shooting, guarding, scoring);
- Aerobic dancing (basic routines); gymnastics (spotting);
- Cross-country (conditioning, long jump, broad jump);
- Calisthenics (body building and muscle toning);
- Archery (notching, drawing and stringing bow, stance, aiming);
- Golf (grip, stance, addressing the ball, swing);
- Yoga (breathing, posture, exercise routines);
- Track and field (dashes, long races, relays);
- Swimming and diving—if pool is available;
- Weight control and maintenance;
- Endurance, suppleness, balance, strength, coordination;
- Career education (sportscasting, officiating, playing).

Grades 11-12

Coming into the class a student should demonstrate knowledge of:

- Lifetime individual and team sports;
- Conditioning activities;
- Value of physical well-being;
- Career opportunities in the field.

In the class students are taught:

- Honing of technique and skill in all sports;
- Dancing and rhythmic movement; aerobic routines;
- Advanced routines for developing and maintaining endurance, strength, speed, suppleness, balance, coordination;
- Squad work, floor exercises, apparatus work;

- Advanced skills in all areas of physical education;
- Swimming — if pool is available;
- Career possibilities in the field;
- Respect for physical fitness;
- Good sportsmanship; respect for equipment.

Chapter 13

SCIENCE IN THE CLASSROOM

OVERVIEW

A basic goal of the science curriculum is to assist students in the use and understanding of the scientific method. From the earliest grades students are taught to observe closely, to compare and contrast and to conduct experiments to see how things work. Safety is taught and stressed. Students acquire knowledge about the way the world works, who and what lives in and on it, what its place is in the universe and what the natural laws are that govern it. Computers are used when and where they are available. The order in which things are presented may differ from one system to another.

Grade K—Students are taught: names of the bodily senses; how the senses are used; how to observe and describe objects and noted changes; properties of water and how it works for us; care of plants and animals; differences between living and non-living objects; how to conduct simple experiments.

Grade 1—Students are taught: distinguishing characteristics of living and non-living things; how to investigate the environment; effects of air and water on the environment; how all people are alike and how everyone differs from everyone else; properties and vocabulary of time; factors necessary for good health; how to conduct simple experiments.

Grade 2—Students are taught: properties and vocabulary of sound, including tone, waves, sonar, loudness, softness; qualities of light and shadow, force and friction; the causes and effects of weather; life cycles of animals and plants and their interdependence; differences among animals including how and where they live and what they need to survive; essential steps in conducting experiments.

Grade 3—Students are taught: properties of rocks and soil; what is learned from soil layers; effects of heating and cooling on matter; how and why thermometers are used; centigrade and Fahrenheit; features and interaction of sun, earth, moon, stars, planets, constellations; space travel; static and circuit electricity; conductors and insulators; safety rules for using electricity; adaptation and behavior of animals and plants in their environments; interdependence of animals, plants and humans; importance of observation in experimentation.

Grade 4—Students are taught: history of earth's changing surface; how to use maps, globes and charts to obtain information; forces that cause changes; properties and vocabulary of light including: reflection, refraction, lenses, lasers, waves; weather and atmospheric conditions; use of measuring instruments for weather: how to record data; forecasting; populations and communities; properties and vocabulary of simple and compound machines including: force, direction, distance, speed, power; food chains and webs; human impact on environment; classification of plants and animals; data collection in experiments.

Grade 5—Students are taught: characteristics and importance of oceans, waves, tides, currents, ocean floors and ocean life forms; structure and function of the sense organs of the human body; human digestive, circulatory, respiratory and excretory systems; a balanced diet; harmful effects of tobacco, alcohol and drugs on the body systems; constellations and gallaxies; series and parallel circuits; magnetic fields of force; electric current; specific characteristics of the scientific method and its reliance on experimentation.

Grade 6—Students are taught: Newton's laws of motion; the effects of gravity and other forces on mass; structure and conservation of matter; classification of substances of living things; fossils and what they have taught us about gelogical change; plant, animal and protist microorganisms; conservation of energy; natural resources and ecology; reproduction and heredity in living things; learning and reasoning processes in lower animals and in humans; observation and data collection as essentials in the scientific method.

Grade 7—Students are taught: causes and effects of interaction of energy and matter; scientific method of problem solving; measuring matter; forms and changes of matter; energy, work and motion; waves including light, sound, water; science and technology; conversion of metric units within the metric system; the use and construction of the periodic table; Newton's laws of motion; work and power; magnetism; radiant energy; conduct of experiments.

From the eighth through the twelfth grade, students are usually allowed to choose which courses they will take and in some cases students opt not to take any more science. Not all schools offer all the courses described here. Some offer more, some less. Most science courses include regular laboratory experience in which students have the opportunity to conduct experiments, learn to use the tools and equipment for conducting research and learn to keep records of their observations. Prediction, theory, trial and error, modeling, simulation, inductive and deductive reasoning and safety rules are stressed.

LIFE SCIENCE—Emphasis is placed on: methods of studying living things; characteristics of living things; use of simple and compound microscopes; life functions; structure and functions of cells; observing cells under microscope; physical, biological and ecological environments; changes in nature; conservation and natural resources; survey of the plant kingdom and the animal kingdom; beginning of life on the earth; heredity and genes; the scientific method.

EARTH SCIENCE—Emphasis is placed on: understanding the environment on a local and a cosmic level; the universe, the solar system and the earth including theories of creation and destruction; surface features of the earth and the processes which are responsible for the formation of these features; meteorology; oceanography; plate tectonics; scientific method.

PHYSICAL SCIENCE—Emphasis is placed on: understanding matter, energy, forces, and motion; more intense study of light, sound, electricity, magnetism; investigation of the earth sciences; study of interaction of the physical and the living world; ecosystems and communities; the human organism; environmental problems; consumer science; current events in science; use and importance of the scientific method.

BIOLOGY—Emphasis is placed on: understanding and defining the differences between "facts" and "theories"; classification of plants and animals; ecology; bioenergetics; cells; functioning of plants and animals; reproduction and genetics; evolution; use of scientific biological techniques for studying living things.

ADVANCED BIOLOGY—Emphasis is on studying: characteristics of life; origin of life; chemistry of life and life forms; celular bases of life; reproduction; genetics; development; normalities and abnormalaties; mutations; differentiation; growth and repair.

CHEMISTRY—Emphasis is on: understanding the chemistry of the conservation of matter and energy (stoichiometry); atomic structure and the periodic chart; molecular structure and bonding of molecules; writing and balancing chemical equations; using formulas; electro-chemistry, oxidation and reduction; energy changes in chemical systems; the chemistry of solids, liquids, gasses, acids, bases and solutions; kinetics and equilibrium; nuclear chemistry; carbon chemistry.

ADVANCED CHEMISTRY—Emphasis is on: details of the periodic chart; redox stoichiometry; laws of gasses, concentrations and solutions; collegiative properties; the acid-base chart; rate law; solutions and equilibrium; synthetics; chemical analysis; organic and inorganic nomenclature; thermodynamics; kinetics; oxidation; instrumentation.

PHYSICS—Emphasis is on: understanding degrees of precision and of variations; observing and investigating motion; motion in the heavens; mechanics; electromagnetism, gravity and light; the atom, the nucleus and energy.

ADVANCED PHYSICS—Students explore: Newtonian mechanics; energetics; oscillations; classical electricity and magnetism; history of modern physics; Einsteinian relativity; photons; atomic models; quantum mechanics; nuclear stability.

SCIENCE IN THE CLASSROOM

Grade K

Coming into the grade a student should:

- Respond to pictures as symbols of people and things;
- Observe changes in materials and substances;
- Sustain interest for a reasonable period of time;
- Listen to directions and perform simple tasks.

In the grade students are taught to:

- Describe and demonstrate use of five senses and parts of body;
- Classify objects by color, shape and size;
- Describe texture and position of objects;
- Demonstrate how forces can change objects (push-pull);
- Measure materials; observe how liquid occupies space;
- Observe how water changes when heated and cooled; how it moves

upward and downward; how objects float and sink; how water dissolves some substances; observe evaporation and condensation;
- Describe weather; relate weather to activities and clothing;
- Distinguish between living and non-living things;
- Observe what plants and animals need to survive;
- Observe similarity between living things and their offspring;
- Observe properties of rocks and soils.

Grade 1

Coming into the grade a student should be able to:

- Describe different kinds of weather;
- Distinguish between living and non-living things.

In the grade students are taught to:

- Classify objects by color, shape, size, texture, weight;
- Sequence yesterday, today, tomorrow, days of the week, months of the year, four seasons; use metric measures;
- Describe relative position of objects (under, over, near, far, here, there); recognize the effects of pollution;
- Identify mountain, valley, forest, plain, dessert, shore;
- Recognize the impact of climate on humans, animals, plants;
- Observe that air takes up space, has weight, moves things;
- Observe water's forms (solid, liquid, gas);
- Observe how plants and animals use water and air;
- Identify types of shelter (humans and other animals);
- Identify the four basic food groups; plan a balanced meal;
- Use techniques of observation and experimentation.

Grade 2

Coming into the grade a student should be able to:

- Classify objects as living or non-living; understand the relationships of time; describe differences in environments;
- Describe characteristics of plants and animals;
- Use metric measures.

In the grade students are taught to:

- Identify and compare sounds (pitch, volume);
- Use materials to transmit, block (shadow) and reflect light;

- Identify different weather conditions and describe seasonal changes and how they affect living;
- Observe how force changes shape, size, speed, direction of objects; friction as a force;
- Recognize interdependence of living organisms;
- Identify in animals: life cycle, respiration, ingestion (and food gathering), excretion, growth, movement;
- Identify in plants: life cycles, functions, parts;
- Use metric measures (liters, degrees Celsius, centimeters, meters); use techniques of observation and experimentation;
- Observe shore ecology; results of wind and wave action.

Grade 3

Coming into the grade a student should be able to:

- Understand basic concepts of light, sound and motion;
- Understand basic weather information and effect of weather on oceans, beaches, animals, plants;
- Use basic measurement tools with understanding.

In the grade students are taught:

- To identify and describe properties of rocks and soil;
- To describe characteristics of matter (takes up space, has weight, responsive to heat and cold—melts, boils, evaporates, expands, contracts, condenses, solidifies);
- Matter contains particles which have positive or negative charges; static and current electricity; conductors and insulators; magnets and magnetism; poles; uses of magnets;
- The universe contains our solar system with its planets and moons; the sun as the source of light and heat; space and space exploration; constellations; measuring techniques;
- Plant and animal adaptation to changing environments;
- Techniques of observation and experimentation.

Grade 4

Coming into the grade a student should be able to:

- Classify rocks by their properties; describe soil layers;
- Recognize solid, gaseous and liquid states of matter;
- Compare and measure energy sources;

- Understand basic theories of electricity and magnetism;
- Identify and name component parts of our solar system.

In the grade students are taught:

- Earth's composition (crust, mantle, core, plates); changes due to continental drift, earthquakes, volcanos, erosion, warming, pollution); winds and directions in which they blow;
- Properties and uses of light (direction and speed of travel, reflection, refraction, color, spectrum, lasers);
- How machines work (a force moving an object through a distance, mechanical advantage, inclined planes, levers, pulleys, screws, wedges, wheels, axles, gears); impact;
- Qualities of communities; producers, consumers, decomposers; food chains and food webs (herbivores, carnivores, omnivores); interdependence of populations; human impact on other plant and animal communities; threat of extinction;
- Conservation as an ecological necessity;
- Use of various kinds of measuring devices; graphing;
- Techniques of observation and experimentation.

Grade 5

Coming into the grade a student should be able to:

- Understand forces effecting change in the earth's surface;
- Understand how winds are generated and how they blow;
- Discuss use of the wheel, axle and gears in machines;
- Describe the basic properties of light;
- Describe food chains and food webs;
- Conduct experiments and demonstrations;
- Read and interpret charts, diagrams and graphs.

In the grade students are taught:

- To measure using millimeters, centimeters, meters; to graph obtained data; to read a tide table;
- Basics of oceans (waves, currents, tides, ocean floor geography, ridges, trenches, sediment, life at levels);
- Sources of fresh water; evaporation; desalinization; rain;

In the grade students are taught:

- Sound sources (direction, speed, intensity, pitch, frequency); telegraph, telephone, phonograph, radio, sonar; music; voice; decibels, vibrations, echoes;

- Human physiological systems (skeleto-muscular, digestive, circulatory, respiratory, excretory); use of food and oxygen; enzymes; effects of diet, exercise and rest; effects of alcohol, drugs and tobacco;
- Aspects of the universe (earth's rotation, revolution and tilt is cause of night, day and seasons); eclipses and phases of moon; stars, constellations and galaxies; light years; radio telescopes;
- Use of a microscope; observation and experimentation methods;
- Qualities of electricity and magnetism (attraction and repulsion); series and parallel circuits; magnetic fields and generation of electric current.

Grade 6

Coming into the grade a student should be able to:

- Discuss evolution of change in earth's surface;
- Explain man's dependence on the oceans and the sun;
- Tell how sound travels and how it is measured;
- Describe the functions of major systems of the human body;
- Classify major bodies of the universe;
- Construct simple electric circuits to produce light, heat;
- Read and interpret basic maps, charts, graphs;
- Conduct and report results of simple experiments.

In the grade students are taught:

- Newton's laws of motion; gravity; mass measured by weight; wing lift by change in air pressure; friction;
- Reading geological maps; fossil formation and dating;
- Structure of matter (atoms, molecules, elements, compounds);
- Microorganisms (cell, amoeba, paramecia, algae, fungi, bacteria, viruses); symbiosis;
- Nature of energy (non-renewable); conservation; pollution;
- Reproduction (terminology: one-parent, two-parent); heredity (dominant and recessive traits, chromosomes, genes, sex-linked traits, selective breeding, mutations, environmental effects); population growth (overcrowding);
- Use of learning and reasoning; scientific method.

The grades in which particular science courses are offered after grade six differ from one school system to another. The particular sequence described below is typical.

Grade 7: Interaction of Energy and Matter

Coming into the class a student should demonstrate:

- Basic knowledge of math and its application to problems;
- Basic understanding of the use of measurement tools;
- Knowledge of the meaning of the following terms: matter, inertia, speed, velocity, force, acceleration, thrust, lift, gravity, orbit, revolution, axis, rotation eclipse, ellipse, properties, elements, compound, mixture, molecule, atom, models, formula, combustion, acid, base, indicator, mass.

In the grade students are taught:

- Techniques of the scientific method of problem solving (observing, classifying, imagining, hypothesizing, criticizing, comparing, assuming, summarizing, interpreting, measuring, collecting data, organizing, problem solving);
- How to read and understand scientific material;
- How to manipulate laboratory equipment safely;
- Modeling as used by the scientist;
- Matter, its forms and changes;
- Energy and electricity for work and motion; waves;
- Use and construction of the periodic table;
- Newton's laws of motion; use of simple machines;
- Laws of conservation of mass and energy; power;
- Radiant energy and its effect on our lives;
- Construction of lab reports based on collected data;
- Use of standard and metric measures; conversions;
- Availability and attractiveness of scientific careers.

Grade 8: Life Science

Coming into the class a student should demonstrate:

- Ability to read science text for the grade;
- Ability to measure in standard and metric systems;
- Ability to perform basic mathematic processes;
- Ability to use standard laboratory equipment.

In the class students are taught:

- Characteristics of living things; the four life functions;
- Use of compound microscope; preparation of wet mount slides;
- Methods of collection and evaluation of data;
- How to prepare a lab report;
- How to construct graphs from collected data;
- How to use dissecting instruments;
- Use of a "control" in scientific investigation;
- Difference between a hypothesis and a theory;
- Metabolism; parts of a cell; life functions and reproduction of a cell;
- Ecology; human impact on the biosphere; producers, consumers and the physical environment; soil, air and water and how they impact on human life; interaction between living things and the environment; balance of nature;
- Major differences between plants and animals; methods of classifying living things;
- Sources of energy; ability of plants to produce their own food and what they need to accomplish food production;
- The five eras of geologic time; theories of evolution;
- Heredity and the function of genes; DNA and RNA;
- Characteristics of individuals—similarities and differences;
- Careers in science.

Grades 8-9: Earth Science

Coming into the class a student should demonstrate:

- Ability to read and understand a science text;
- Ability to compute with understanding;
- Familiarity with basics of biological and physical sciences.

In the class students are taught:

- Characteristics of universe, solar system, earth;
- The essence of earth's dependence on the sun; seasons;
- The effects the moon has on the earth; phases of the moon;
- Difference between stars and planets;
- How time is kept on earth;
- How rocks are formed; rocks and minerals; erosion; soil;
- Formation of land forms; earthquakes; plate tectonics; surface features of earth; meteorology; oceanography; tides; winds; weather; climate; topography and topographic maps;
- Careers.

Grade 9: Physical Science

Coming into the class a student should demonstrate ability to:

- Solve simple algebraic problems; compute ratios;
- Read a grade level text with comprehension;
- Recall information from basic elementary science courses.

In the class students are taught:

- The value of observation, investigation and analysis as tools of the scientist;
- How to use measuring devices appropriately and accurately;
- How to construct graphs from collected data;
- To recognize the basic properties of matter and energy;
- How force creates motion;
- Characteristics of light and sound and their impact on living things;
- Electricity and magnetism and how we use them;
- The interaction of the living and the non-living on earth;
- Ecosystems and communities; environments; consumer science;
- Characteristics of the human organism;
- Career opportunities in the sciences.

Grades 9–10: Biology

Coming into the class a student should demonstrate ability to:

- Read a biology text with understanding;
- Apply basic math skills to solving problems;
- Construct and interpret graphs;
- Recall information presented in elementary science courses.

In the class students are taught:

- Use of the metric system; use of laboratory equipment;
- How organisms interact in their search for energy and space;
- Methods of classification of living things based on their structural similarities; modeling;
- Evolution and how creatures evolved from earlier life forms;
- Biogenesis—concept accepted by most scientists today;
- Living things are constructed of atoms and molecules;
- Cells make up all living things; cells run on energy;
- Energy flows from the sun through the biosphere;

- Photosynthesis (the process by which plants turn sunlight and water into sugar) is basic to all life on earth;

In the class students are taught:

- Respiration (an aerobic process) is a series of chemical reactions which break down foodstuffs and release energy and is controlled by enzymes;
- Asexual and sexual reproductive mechanisms and processes;
- The structure and control function of DNA;
- The basic laws of genetics and how to use them; the effects of heredity and environment on organisms; mutation and evolution;
- Human behavior and future evolution;
- General structure and function of systems in living things;
- Cause and effect of behavior of living things;
- Bacteriology, microbiology, botany, zoology, anatomy, physiology, biochemistry, biophysics;
- Scientific and science related careers.

Grade 10: Chemistry

Coming into the class a student should demonstrate ability to:

- Use basic lab techniques and the scientific method;
- Work with understanding in the metric system;
- Compute and deal with equations;
- Read a text with understanding.

In the class students are taught:

- Laboratory skills pertinent to chemistry;
- Techniques of problem solving; use of the periodic chart;
- Basic atomic and molecular structure and its relationship to bonding and energy changes; atomic and molecular architecture;
- The three phases of matter (solid, liquid, gas);
- Factors affecting solubility and solution processes; specific concentrations in preparation of solutions;
- Acid-base theory; modeling;
- Balancing equations and predicting changes; factors determining the type and rate of chemical change; effect of adding energy on chemical change; kinetics;
- Equilibrium, reaction rate and extent of reaction;

- Oxidation, reduction, galvanic and electrolytic cells; carbon chemistry;
- Career opportunities in the field.

Grades 11–12: Physics

Coming into the class a student should demonstrate ability to:

- Perform mathematical operations with exponents;
- Solve simple algebraic equations and ratios;
- Use the metric system;
- Construct and interpret graphs.

In the class students are taught:

- Concepts and laws of motion—straight and curved; free-fall; circular orbit; simple harmonic motion;
- Newtonian mechanics—linear and rotational; gravitational fields; inertial and non-inertial frames of reference; mechanical resonance;
- Gravitational inverse square law;
- Center of mass, linear momentum; conservation of linear momentum with appropriately isolated systems; elasticity of collisions leading to exponential decay curve;
- Work and energy; mechanical energy and energetics; conditions for conservation of mechanical energy; mechanical energy and free-fall; conservation of energy and mass in appropriately isolated systems; relativistic considerations;
- Future energy sources;
- Kinetic theory of matter; temperature and internal energy; conducted heat; first and second laws of thermodynamics; variational principles; mechanical waves, sound and the behavior of light; duality of electromagnetic radiation;
- Electric and magnetic fields; electric charge; quantization of simple DC and AC electricity; electromagnetic waves;
- Models of the atom; duality of electromagnetic radiation and of matter; Heisenberg uncertainty principle; Pauli exclusion principle;
- The nucleus; nuclear field; nuclear models; fission; fusion; radioactivity; Quark hypothesis; presumed safe levels of radiation dosage;
- Methods of working with a lab partner;
- Career opportunities in the field.

Grades 11-12: Advanced Chemistry

Coming into the class a student should demonstrate ability to:

- Use scientific techniques;
- Understand use of periodic chart; balance chemical equations;
- Work skillfully in a chemistry laboratory;
- Respond with accuracy to questions covering work done in basic chemistry course and basic physics.

In the class students are taught:

- Stoichiometry; energy changes; atomic structure; molecular orbitals; hybrid atomic orbitals;
- Periodicity; structure and bonding; isomerism;
- Formulae and equations; energy changes and bonding;
- Electricity and chemistry; equilibrium; oxidation; reduction;
- Solution process; acids and bases; metals;
- Phase equilibria and phase diagrams;
- Carbon chemistry; hydrocarbons;
- Gas laws; kinetic theory related to gases, liquids, solids;
- Nuclear chemistry; fission; fusion;
- Career opportunities in the field.

Grade 12: Advanced Biology

Coming into the class a student should demonstrate ability to:

- Follow laboratory procedures;
- Express observations and graph results;
- Respond accurately to questions testing what was learned in the basic biology course.

Information and skills to be presented in the class include:

- Methods of developing and testing hypotheses;
- Chemical and cellular basis of life forms; origins of life; characteristics of life; reproduction; genetics; development; differentiation; growth and repair;
- Conceptualizing; classifying; analyzing; interpreting;
- Induction and deduction; laboratory projects;
- Ecology; environmental influences on biology;
- Drugs, medicines and chemicals and their effects;
- Career opportunities in the field.

Grade 12: Advanced Physics

Coming into the class a student should demonstrate ability to:

- Follow laboratory procedures;
- Express observations and graph results; solve trigonometric equations; solve complex algebraic problems;
- Respond accurately to questions testing what was learned in the basic physics course.

Information and skills to be presented in the class include:

- Learning to use sensitive, delicate lab equipment; working independently on problems;
- Newtonian mechanics (linear and rotational); moments of inertia;
- Energetics; oscillations; electricity and magnetism; reduced mass; angular momentum; inverse-square orbiting; Doppler effect; Carnot cycle; isothermal and adiabatic processes;
- Classical physics and its inadequacies; Coulomb's and Gauss's laws; capacitors and dielectrics; electric vectors; Ohm's law; resistors in series and parallel; Kirchoff's theorems; Biot-Savart's and Ampere's laws; meters and motors; electromagnetic induction; transformers; wave propagation; optics; behavior of light; advent of quantum mechanics;
- Einsteinian relativity; time dilation; twin paradox; length contraction and mass increase; conservation of mass and energy;
- The photon and first atomic models; Planck's solution; cathode rays and electrons;
- Rutherford's planetary model; Bohr and the stable atom; Moseley's x-rays; correspondence; DeBroglie's matter waves; Heisenberg's uncertainty principle; pair production annihilation; antimatter; spectral line broadening; Doppler broadening; Pauli's exclusion principle; Hartree's atomic model; atomic energy states; energy bands; nuclear stability; Becquerel; the Curies; heavy isotopes; emissions; Lee and Yang; parity; nuclear shell model;
- Quark hypothesis; classes of particles; detectors of radioactivity; dosage units and limits; transmutations; fission and fusion; stellar evolution;
- Career opportunities in the field.

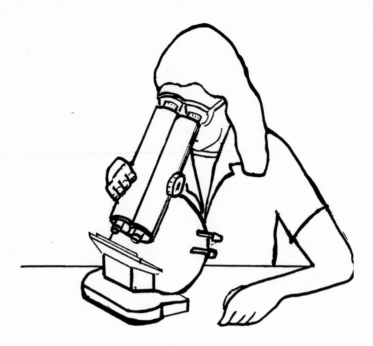

Chapter 14

SOCIAL STUDIES IN THE CLASSROOM

OVERVIEW

The group of subjects known as the social studies include courses in the history and geography of the world, examinations of civilization and civic behavior, sociology, anthropology, politics, economics, psychology, nationalism, patriotism, war, peace, ecology and the human condition. From the earliest grades students are taught what is and is not acceptable social behavior. In every grade instruction is offered in the major concepts of the subject areas making up the social studies.

Grade K—Students are taught to: recognize land and water masses on maps and globes; listen and speak in discussions with classmates; name and identify celebrations appropriate to significant holidays; sing holiday songs; develop good manners; understand safety rules; recognize community helpers and the jobs they do.

Grade 1—Students are taught to: construct and use simple maps; recognize locations on globes; appreciate human and other animal family relationships; understand differences in family practices from one culture to another; understand roles of community helpers and the importance of local community resources; use the concepts of seasons, months, holidays; listen to simple stories related to American history; memorize words and meaning of the pledge of allegiance.

Grade 2—Students are taught: Symbols for landforms and water bodies on maps and globes; to find and identify the United States; to sing the national anthem; the three basic human needs—clothing, food and shelter; their relation to human survival; how humans in varied environments on earth provide for these basic needs; the impact of transportation and communication on various cultures; to do simple fact-finding research and write brief reports; the qualities of duty, citizenship, leadership, independence and interdependence.

Grade 3—Students are taught: map skills including use of legends, scales, color interpretations, hemispheres; location of home state, county, city or town; locating and using information found in a dictionary, glossary, almanac, encyclopedia, atlas; the geography, history and economic development of specific communities; contributions of native Americans and immigrant groups, to the culture of America; interdependence of persons and communities; the student's neighborhood as a community; rights and responsibilities of a citizen in a community.

Grade 4—Students are taught: use of maps to identify ocean currents, sea levels, weather, political subdivisions, elevations; the variety in typical regions of the earth regarding landforms, climate, culture, government, natural resources, occupations and their interdependence; the impact on human culture of living in forests, deserts, plains, mountains and near or in oceans (on islands); the history and geography of the home state; use of an encyclopedia and almanac; how to take notes and prepare outlines; some research techniques including crediting sources, using the library, interviewing.

Grade 5—Students are taught: use of maps to trace journeys of early explorers of America; concepts of longitude and latitude, time zones, equator, polar regions, Tropic of Cancer and Tropic of Capricorn; a basic overview of history of the United States; basic concepts of democratic government; contributions of many great men and women to American history; likenesses and differences of major sections of the country in geography, history and culture; names, capitals, major cities and major natural resources of each of the United States; research and study skills.

Grade 6—Students are taught: routes of the explorers of Latin America and Canada; reversal of seasons and change in air and water circulation patterns in Southern Hemisphere; cultural impact of equatorial and polar climate; history, geography, and variety of cultures found in Latin America and Canada; to locate, name and identify the geographical features, natural resources and economic development of major areas of Latin America and Canada; colonialism, regionalism, revolution and politics in Canada and Latin America; comparison and contrast with similar happenings in American history; basic study skills including note taking.

In the secondary grades, courses are offered by name, since each school system has its own grade placement and sequence for them.

Course names may differ but course content, taken as a whole, will be similar from one system to another.

WORLD HISTORY I—Students will focus on: study of primative societies and the evolution to early civilizations and great cultures of the past; the geography, civilization, culture, religion and mythology of ancient Egypt, Greece, Mesopotamia, Rome, China, India and medieval Europe; outstanding historical events of each era: group and independent study skills.

WORLD HISTORY II—Students will focus on: history of the world from the Renaissance through the twentieth century; transition from medieval culture to the Renaissance; rise of politically separate European nation states; the industrial revolution and its global impact; colonialism and its global impact from inception to today; governmental styles including: monarchy, democracy, fascism, socialism, communism; wars, their causes and effects; compromise and conciliation; cultural, political, economic, social, technological and scientific developments influencing modern history; group and independent study skills.

UNITED STATES HISTORY I—Focus will be on: early continental development from the original colonizations through the French and Indian War up to and including the American Revolution and establishment of the United States of America; documents of democracy including Articles of Confederation, Declaration of Independence, American Constitution, Bill of Rights; post-revolutionary period and aspects of American growth; conditions leading to the American Civil War; American Civil War; contributions of women and ethnic minorities to American growth.

UNITED STATES HISTORY II—Focus will be on: post Civil War reconstruction and legacies it left; development of the frontier; opening the continent; Spanish American War; American involvement in world wars; waves of immigration; American transformation from a rural agrarian to an urban industrial society; development of atomic and nuclear weapons; League of Nations and United Nations; Korean and Vietnam Wars; politics and countervailing powers; war and peace periods; modern economics.

ECONOMICS—Focus will be on: scope and history of economic theory and famous economists; concepts of economic geography; concepts of gross national product, money supply, free market competition, government controls, taxes and tariffs, cooperatives and common markets; banking systems and federal reserve; production and distribution of goods and services; supply and demand and free enterprise; land, labor, capital, management, unions, conglomerates, monopolies; liberalism; conservatism; depression, inflation, recession, public debt; deficits and national budget; stocks, bonds, commodities and securities and exchange commission.

Some school systems offer additional courses which focus on specific and/or periodic aspects of history, geography, economics, psychology or sociology and probe more extensively into these areas than is possible in the survey courses described above. Such courses are generally electives and may include:

- History of the twentieth century from World War II to today including: wars (hot and cold); social movements; emerging democracies; revolutions; economic rivalries; spheres of influence; the influence of atomic and nuclear energy.
- World studies including: contemporary survey of regions and cultures; Arab-Israeli conflict; Middle East wars; Central American wars; South Asian conflicts; India-Pakistan feuds; Pan-Americanism; South Africa and apartheid; iron curtain and cold war; start of its demise; armament and disarmament.
- Modern European History including: political geography, history and religion of Europe from Renaissance to today; cultural, political, economic, monarchial and social development; "isms" including: absolutism, imperialism, colonialism, nationalism, socialism, fascism, communism; growth of republics; causes, issues, impacts and effects of European and world wars; the cold war and iron curtain; events in today's Europe.
- Economic Geography
- Contemporary Society
- The Theory of Knowledge
- History of Minorities
- History of Women
- Psychology
- Sociology
- Civics
- The Humanities

SOCIAL STUDIES IN THE CLASSROOM

Grade K

Coming into the grade a student should:

- Be able to listen and respond to simple directions;
- Tell an experience to group; enter discussion with peers;
- Sustain interest for a reasonable period of time;
- Understand the concept of major holidays;
- Recognize colors.

In the grade students are taught to:

- Recognize the globe as a model of the earth; distinguish land and water areas;
- Listen critically and retain main idea;
- Exchange ideas with teacher and peers;
- Take part in show and tell;
- Ask questions relating to shared experiences;
- Develop understanding of time system, calendar, seasons;
- Exhibit social skills including: cooperating, sharing, taking turns, listening, respecting rights of others; learning and obeying rules;
- Put events into appropriate sequence;
- Recite some rhymes and sing some holiday and seasonal songs;
- Recite the pledge of allegiance.

Grade 1

Coming into the grade a student should be able to:

- Identify land and water areas on the globe;
- Sequence events or a series of pictures accurately;
- Accept responsibility for completion of a task;
- Respect the rights of others; be courteous;
- Tell something about each of the major holidays;
- Understand simple concepts of time and calendar;
- Understand and obey the school rules.

In the grade students are taught:

- *Map skills including:* relationship between the way the earth turns and day and night; how to use a map to find direction; how to trace a route on a neighborhood map; how to understand some map symbols;
- *Research skills including:* using a table of contents to find information; alphabetizing on the first letter; composing titles for a story, picture, chart; arranging events in sequence; classifying pictures and events under main headings;

In the grade students are taught:

- *Social skills including:* the importance of protecting and preserving personal and public property; rules of conduct for classroom and school behavior; respecting the rights of others; accepting responsibility for completion of a task;
- *Computer skills:* drill and practice with appropriate computer-assisted instruction programs;
- *The family including:* characteristics of human and animal families; how families differ from other groups; family patterns (single parent, etc.); the immediate and the extended family; likenesses and differences in families from other parts of the world; family changes; how community helpers assist families (doctors, nurses, dentists, police, teachers, etc.); people's basic needs;
- *Holidays including:* special historic events; international events; birthdays; elementary use of a calendar;
- *Patriotism including:* The pledge of allegiance and the "Star-Spangled Banner."

Grade 2

Coming into the grade a student should be able to:

- Identify land and water areas on a map and globe;
- Relate events in proper sequence;
- Classify things into general categories (animals, food, shelter, etc.);
- Accept responsibility for the completion of a task;
- Recognize characteristics of family units;
- Identify basic holidays and understand why we celebrate them;
- Recite the pledge of allegiance and sing the "Star-Spangled Banner."

In the grade students are taught:

- *Map skills including:* how to identify and name the major kinds of land forms and water bodies of earth; how to associate major climate regions with specific areas on a globe; how to use symbols to find cities, rivers, mountains; how to find the United States on a globe and on a flat map;
- *Research skills including:* sequencing yesterday, today, tomorrow, days of week, months of year, four seasons; use of calendar; use of table of contents; reading to find answers to questions; collecting information on a single topic;

In the grade students are taught:

- *Social skills including:* how and why people live in groups; sharing; understanding and obeying rules; leadership and its qualities; improving self-confidence in speaking before a group; making choices and selecting options; respecting opinions of others; practicing cooperation and control;
- *Food including:* how and why food supply is basic to survival; how food preference is based on tradition, availability, cost; how different peoples prepare and eat food differently; food groups and foods which help build healthy bodies;
- *Clothing including:* how clothing is determined by climate, personal preference, occupation and custom; influence of weather on clothing choices; styles;
- *Shelter including:* how homes differ depending on climate, available materials, space and customs; the kinds of workers involved in the building of a house; names for different types of houses;
- *Transportation and communication including:* how and why the world keeps seeming to shrink;

- How to write a simple report (one or two sentences);
- How to do assigned tasks on a computer.

Grade 3

Coming into the grade a student should:

- Use maps and globes to locate rivers, oceans, lakes, cities, mountains, the United States;
- Display confidence talking before a group;
- Appreciate how food, clothing and shelter are basic human needs; discuss how and why leadership is necessary in group situations;
- Identify various means of transportation and communication available to us in the modern world.

In the grade students are taught:

- *Map skills including:* hemispheres; north, south, east and west; recognizing particular kinds of land and water areas (bays, islands, peninsulas, lakes, rivers, seas, continents, countries, etc.); determining distance; colors used for specific purposes; relief maps; location of hometown; nearest city, state of residence, bounding states;

In the grade students are taught:

- *Research skills including:* how to prepare simple oral and written reports; use of a glossary and an index; meaning of commonly used abbreviations; how to use the library to find information; computer review of vocabulary;
- *Social skills including:* increased sense of responsibility; increased ability and skill in self-direction and independence; consistent use of basic rules of courtesy; increased ability to plan and work with others in accomplishing tasks;
- *Characteristics of communities including:* the impact of its geography on how people live; trade; mining; transportation; farming and other human-use factors; interdependence of communities; economic and cultural development of communities; native and immigrant groups and their contributions; our country as a multi-ethnic community; likenesses and differences among ethnic groups; responsibility of the citizen in a community; the history of civilization is the combined history and interaction of communities;
- *Our town including:* local government; town history; surrounding towns; local facilities; location of town on a map.

Grade 4

Coming into the grade a student should:

- Use symbols and legends to identify places on maps and globes;
- Show ability to prepare simple oral and written reports;
- Use a variety of sources for gathering information;
- Be familiar with history and geography of the local area;
- Understand and use the rules of courtesy and obey school rules.

In the grade students are taught:

- *Map and globe skills including:* use of grid lines; use of color to indicate elevations and depths or political subdivisions; location of state and national boundaries; major political and physical areas of home state;
- *Research skills including:* creating time lines; interviewing as a way of gathering information; crediting sources on written reports; use of glossary, index, table of contents, encyclopedia; outlining;

In the grade students are taught:

- *Social skills including:* parliamentary procedure; elements of fair play and sportsmanship; citizenship; using consensus to reach agreement; distinguishing between work done successfully by individuals and work done more successfully by groups;
- *Characteristics of regions:* definition of a region; similarities and differences among regions with reference to climate, landforms, culture, occupations, human and natural resources, governments; characteristics of forest regions (rain, mild climate, raw materials, animal and plant life); desert regions (dry, extreme temperature variations between day and night, sparsely populated, specialized adaptations of plant and animal life); farming regions; mountain regions; cities; ocean regions;
- *Home state:* history and geography; government;
- *Culture:* heritage of peoples who live in home state.

Grade 5

Coming into the grade a student should:

- Recognize and use political and physical maps and globes;
- Use simple parliamentary procedure;
- Prepare written and oral reports;

- Understand regional similarities and differences;
- Know the history and geography and cultural heritage of the people of the home state.

In the grade students are taught:

- *Geography and map and globe skills including:* routes used by the explorers of America; geographic influences on the development of the nation; locating areas of historical significance; locating our country with reference to other places in the world; locating physical features on a map of the United States; understanding time zones, latitude and longitude; study of major American regions (New England, Middle Atlantic, Southeast, North Central, South Central, Rocky Mountain, Pacific).

In the grade students are taught:

- *Research skills including:* skimming for information; recognizing main ideas; working with historical time lines; distinguishing different points of view; creating bulletin boards with charts, graphs, cartoons; dramatizing historical events; preparing and presenting oral and written reports; reporting on current events;
- *Social skills including:* contributing ideas and accepting constructive criticism; planning; making decisions based on data; responding to individual differences with sensitivity; helping newcomers to the group; rights and responsibilities of citizenship; using a computer in simulations;
- *Introduction to America including:* before the European explorers arrived; explorations; settlements; history and development; freedom and independence; democratic principles; the Constitution and the Bill of Rights; contributions of great persons (men, women and minorities of both sexes) to the growth of America;
- *Current events.*

Grade 6

Coming into the grade a student should be able to:

- Skim material to find basic ideas;
- Accomplish independent research; plan class projects;
- Use maps and globes with understanding;
- Respond knowingly to questions on basic facts concerning American history and geography.

In the grade students are taught:

- *Geography and map and globe skills including:* routes of explorers and settlers in Canada and Latin America; methods of computing distances using both miles and kilometers; uses of special-purpose maps; longitude and latitude;
- *Research skills including:* outlining; taking notes from oral and written sources; preparing and presenting oral and written reports; using card catalogue in the library, table of contents and indexes to find information; computer use;
- *Social skills:* increasing insights into rights and feelings of others; coping without conflict; evaluating and using constructive criticism; recognizing and dealing with peer problems; aspects of citizenship;

In the grade students are taught:

- *Latin America and Canada including:* ancient civilizations (Mayas, Incas, Aztecs); European explorers and their exploits in Canada and Latin America; colonialism; struggles for independence; geography, history, climate and politics of the individual entities (Canada, Mexico, Central America, West Indies, Argentina, Bolivia, Brazil, Chile, Columbia, Equador, Guyanas, Paraguay, Peru, Uruguay, Venezuela); lives and works of famous Latin Americans and Canadians;
- *Current events.*

Grade 7: World History I

Coming into the class a student should:

- Be conversant with the basic history and geography of the Western Hemisphere;
- Know how to take notes, outline, organize a notebook, use a library to obtain data, prepare oral and written reports;
- Use maps and globes to obtain information.

In the class students are taught:

- *Geography and civics including:* basic organization of federal, state and local governments; seats of governments including state capitals and county seats; current events and using maps to find locations of happenings;
- *Pre-history including:* prehistoric humans; accomplishments of primatives; primative societies in the twentieth century;

- *Ancient civilizations including:* basic life-styles; myths and folktales; values; writers; philosophers; musicians; artists; special contributions:
  - Greece: art; drama; government; philosophy including idea of individual worth;
  - Rome: order; stability; endurance; rules; materialism; force and ambition to conquer and subdue;
  - American Indian: tribes; philosophies; hardships; art and crafts; accomplishments;
- *Future including:* environmental needs and challenges; governments and their roles.
- *Citizenship including:* rights and responsibilities of individuals in free societies.

Grade 8: World History II

Coming into the class a student should demonstrate:

- Ability to take notes and outline;
- Ability to seek and find information in a library;
- Basic map- and graph-reading skills;
- Ability to act cooperatively in a group;
- Knowledge of the emergence of civilizations and cultures;
- Some ability to project into the future.

In the class students are taught:

- *Geography and civics including:* map identification and various projections; political systems and personalities; basics of federal government and state and local governments; national and international current events and their implications;
- *Skills including:* reading and reporting on a historical novel; to examine history from more than one point of view; to correlate facts from several different sources; to relate history to the present and the future; to read a newspaper;
- *The Middle Ages including:* struggle for survival; emergence of feudalism; characteristics and structure of feudal society;
- *The Renaissance including:* revived interest in classical culture, achievements and inventions; exploration; expansion of trade routes; colonization and its political implications;
- *The Reformation including:* changes in religion; the rise of nations and decline of feudalism; centralizing governments; development of strong monarchies in Europe;

- *The Age of Revolution including:* impact of American and French revolutions on the rest of the world; difference between evolution and revolution;
- *The Industrial Revolution including:* nineteenth century changes in manufacturing from hand to machine processes; invention of labor-saving devices and new techniques of production;
- *The Twentieth Century and the Age of Mass Society including:* wars (World War I, World War II, Korean War, Vietnam) and their consequences; nationalism; socialism; communism; fascism; capitalism; utopianism; imperialism; totalitarianism;
- *The depression including:* effects in America; effects in other nations;
- *Citizenship including:* rights and responsibilities of an individual in a free society; civil rights.

Grades 9–10: United States History I

Coming into the class a student should demonstrate:

- Ability to investigate a topic using good research skills;
- Basic knowledge of world history;
- Basic knowledge of U.S. and world geography and ability to locate countries and major subdivisions on maps and globes;
- Ability to read and understand a newspaper and use it as an information source.

In the class students are taught:

- Details of the exploration and settlement of the American continent by Europeans and nationals from other areas;
- Colonial settlements and their characteristics;
- Causes and outcomes of the French and Indian war;
- Incidents leading up to the American Revolution; the Declaration of Independence; the Articles of Confederation; the Revolution itself;
- The Constitution and the Bill of Rights; the way these two documents affect our lives today;
- The Federalist period and the marks it left on our society;
- Jacksonian Democracy and how it shaped our country;
- Nationalism and Sectionalism—the advocates for each side and the issues which separated them;
- The incidents and beliefs leading up to the Civil War; the war itself; the legacy it left;

- Reconstruction and the problems which emerged; racial tension; the roles of minorities (Indians, Blacks, Mexicans, Irish, Asians, Eastern Europeans); roles of women; contributions of women and minorities to American society;
- The urbanization of American society;
- The rights and responsibilities of citizens in a democracy; voting as a privilege and a responsibility; the importance of staying in touch with current events.

Grades 10–11: United States History II

Coming into the class a student should demonstrate:

- Understanding of the aspects of American history covered in United States History I;
- Understanding of the American Constitution and the Bill of Rights;

Coming into the class a student should demonstrate:

- Ability to respond correctly to questions concerning map skills with reference to the United States;
- Ability to locate and use information in a library;
- Ability to take notes and keep a notebook for study purposes.

In the class students are taught:

- The difference between inductive and deductive reasoning in interpreting historical data; debating skills; comparing and contrasting historical sources;
- Details of the period of Reconstruction after the Civil War; racism; migrations and immigration; industrial growth of the country; the opening of the West;
- Protest movements (agrarian and labor); parties and politics with stress on 1877 through 1893;
- Emerging from isolation; the Spanish-American War; the Open Door Policy; the Monroe Doctrine; foreign policy from 1898 through 1919;
- The progressive movement; waves of immigration;
- World War I—causes and effects; how America became involved; Woodrow Wilson and the League of Nations;
- The twenties and the start of the Great Depression; FDR and the New Deal; the Good Neighbor Policy; economic theories;

- World War II—causes and effects; how America became involved; Truman and the atomic bombs; the United Nations;
- The Cold War and the Iron Curtain; the Korean War; the Vietnam War; New Frontier; Great Society; Nixon years;
- The 1960s, 1970s, 1980s—characteristics of a changing society (culture, values, mores, etc.); patriotism;
- Citizenship including—respect for human dignity; respect for evidence; sense of civic responsibility; individual vs. collective rights;
- Skills including—ability to analyze social problems and discuss relevant facts; ability to organize data; ability to recognize biased statements; ability to select from among alternative interpretations.

Grades 10–12: Electives

In general, secondary school students have a wide variety of elective courses in the social studies from which to choose. Examples of such offerings are listed below. Most schools will not offer all of them.

After having taken survey courses in World History and United States History, electives such as these give the student the opportunity to concentrate on a period in history, an area in geography, an aspect of government or an aspect of human endeavor. Some of them are offered as "honors" courses for students who are academically gifted.

Because they are unique to the system providing them, they are titled below but not further described.

- CIVICS AND GOVERNMENT
- HISTORY OF THE TWENTIETH CENTURY
- CONTEMPORARY WORLD STUDIES
- MODERN EUROPEAN HISTORY
- ECONOMICS AND ECONOMIC GEOGRAPHY
- CONTEMPORARY SOCIETY
- THE THEORY OF KNOWLEDGE
- THE HUMANITIES
- THE HISTORY OF MINORITIES IN AMERICA
- THE HISTORY OF WOMEN
- THIRD WORLD STUDIES
- PSYCHOLOGY
- SOCIOLOGY (and/or) ANTHROPOLOGY

Chapter 15

SPECIAL EDUCATION

The structure below is designed to provide educationally handicapped students with placement in the least restrictive, appropriate
environment while at the same time providing optimum contact with
mainstream classes. The potential for movement into regular classes is
always available.

Steps for developing and implementing an educational program for
students with educational handicaps include:

Identification	By principal, teacher, counselor, parent, other
Referral to child study team	By principal, teacher, counselor, (parent consent needed)
Evaluation	By child study team including psyologist, learning consultant, social worker
Consultation	With nurse, school doctor, speech therapist, psychiatrist, neurologist, other specialists
Classification conference	With special services team, teachers, building administrators, nurse, counselor, parents
Design of individualized educational program	With child study team members, teachers, parents
Program alternatives	Curriculum modification; supplemental instruction, resource room, special education class, out-of-district class, residential, individual
Placement procedures	Program selection, visit by parent and student, application, orientation, enrollment notice, transportation

Follow-up   Evaluation, student progress reports, classroom observation, annual re— view reclassification or declassification

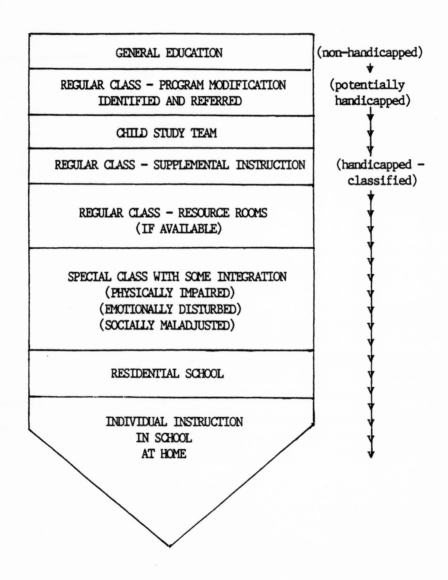

GLOSSARY

A

ABORTION—An ending of the growth of a fetus and its removal from a womb.

ABSOLUTISM—Government by a ruler who has complete power over everything.

ABUSE—Misuse or mistreatment; most frequently stated as "drug abuse."

AC and DC—Used to describe the two different kinds of electric current: alternating current or direct current.

ACADEMIC—Theoretical or literary; generally referring to something scholarly.

ACCELERATION—A speeding up.

ACCELLERANDO—Gradually faster (used as a direction in music).

ACCOMPANIMENT—Join with (usually refers to musical instruments).

ACCRUALS—Something added by periodic growth.

ACETYLENE—Colorless gas used for welding.

ACHIEVE—Accomplish as a result of effort.

ACID—Sour, sharp or biting. In chemistry, the opposite of alkaline or base.

ACRYLICS—A paint made of resin and soluble in water.

ADAPTATION—An adjustment generally made by a living thing so as to fit better into its environment.

ADDICTIVE—Something that makes one dependent on it.

ADDITIVE—A substance which is added to another.

ADIABATIC—Occurring without a loss or gain of heat.

ADJECTIVE—A word that modifies (or expresses something about) a noun, i.e. The *red* dress fits.

ADVERB—A word which modifies a verb, an adjective or another adverb, i.e. She is a *very* tall girl.

ADVOCATES—People who are for a cause of some sort.

AEROBICS—Exercises which fill the body with oxygen.

AESTHETICALLY—Paying attention to the beauty which can be effected.

AESTHETICS—Philosophy of beauty.

AFFIXES—One or more letters added to the beginning or end of a word, i.e. re, er, ing, ed, est.

AGILITY—Ability to move quickly and easily.

AGRARIAN—Relating to farming.

ALGAE—Water plants like seaweed containing chlorophyll but no vein system.

ALGEBRA—A branch of mathematics which uses letters rather than numbers in making calculations.

ALGORISM or ALGORITHM—A procedure in mathematics which helps us calculate. It is what we more generally refer to as an "example."

ALLEGIANCE—Loyalty to a government, a person or a cause.

ALLEGORY—A story about human conduct or experience.

ALMANAC—A yearly publication containing astrological data as well as information on many other topics.

AMOEBA—A one-celled animal.

AMPLITUDE—Fullness. Often refers to radio waves.

ANALOGIES—Ways in which two or more things are alike although they differ in other ways.

ANALYTIC—Examining the parts of something to determine its nature.

ANATOMICAL—Referring to the body or to the structure of an organism.

ANGLE—The space formed when two straight lines meet.

ANGULAR—Containing many angles.

ANNIHILATION—Complete destruction.

ANOREXIA—An illness in which a person eats less and less generally because of a misconception about fatness.

ANTHEM—A song of praise.

ANTHROPOLOGY—The study of humankind from our first appearance on earth through all of our cultures.

ANTONYMS—Words that have opposite meanings.

APARTHEID—A form of government dedicated to keeping people of different races from living together.

APOSTROPHE—A punctuation mark used to express the possessive or to show a missing letter or letters.

APPLICATION—Something placed on a surface.

APPROPRIATE—Suitable.

APPROXIMATE—Nearly correct. Also, estimate.

ARCHITECTURE—The art and science of planning buildings and structures.

ARCS—Curves which are parts of a circle.

AREAS—The amount of surface contained within a boundary.

ARITHMETIC—A branch of mathematics stressing calculating.

ARMAMENT—Military strength.

ARRAYS—Arrangements of objects in a specific order.

ARTICLE—A word used with a noun, i.e. *The* man.

ASCRIBED—Attributed to a supposed cause.

ASEXUAL—Involving no sexual action.

ASSOCIATIVE—A mathematical principle showing the order in which numerals can be combined.

ATLAS—A book of maps.

ATOM—An extremely small particle.

ATOMIC—Referring to the atom.

AUDITORY—Referring to hearing.

AURAL—Relating to the ear.

AUTOBIOGRAPHIES—Books written by the author about his or her own life.

AVAILABLE—Ready to be used.

AVERAGES—About midway between extremes.

AXIOMS—A statement generally accepted as being true.

AXIS—A real or imaginary straight line passing through a body which revolves around it.

B

BACTERIA—A group of microscopic plants, some of which cause disease.

BACTERIOLOGY—Study of bacteria and what they do.

BATIK—Method of hand printing textiles by using wax applications and dyes.

BEARINGS—Machine parts in which other parts turn.

BEVEL—To cut or shape an edge on a slant.

BIBLIOGRAPHY—A list of books, their authors and publishers.

BINOMIAL—A mathematical expression consisting of two terms.

BIOCHEMISTRY—Study accenting the chemistry of living things.

BIOENERGETICS—Relating to energy produced by living organisms.

BIOGENESIS—Development of life from pre-existing life.

BIOGRAPHIES—Stories of the lives of people written by others.

BIOLOGICAL—With reference to the study of living things.

BIOPHYSICS—The physics of living organisms.

BIOSPHERE—That part of the world in which life can exist.

BLUEPRINT—A detailed plan of action.

BONDING—Becoming firmly attached.

BOTANY—Study of plant life.

BRAINSTORMING—Combining ideas offered by members of a group.

BRAZE—Solder with an alloy such as brass.

BULEMIA—An eating disorder in which a person gorges and then regurgitates.

BUSHING—A metal lining used as a bearing.

C

CALCULATING—Mathematical process of figuring numbers.

CALCULUS—A branch of mathematics using symbols and integrals of functions.

CALORIES—Units of measurements of heat produced by food in the human body.

CAMS—A rotating or sliding projection (as on a wheel).

CANCER and CAPRICORN—(Tropics) Parallels of latitude 23.5 degrees north and south of the equator.

CAPACITOR—Energy-storing device.

CAPITALIZATION—Using the capital form of letters.

CAPRICORN—(See CANCER.)

CARBON—A natural element contained in most living tissue.

CARDINAL NUMBERS—(As different from ORDINAL NUMBERS) one, two, three, four, five, six . . . etc.

CARDIOVASCULAR—Referring to the heart and the arteries and veins which contain the blood in the body.

CARNIVORES—Animals which eat other animals (meat) as food.

CATHODE—The negative electrode of a cell.

CELLS—The fundamental building blocks of life containing a nucleus and a surrounding membrane.

CELSIUS—Heat measurement in the metric system.

CENTIGRADE—Measures on a thermometer on which 0 represents freezing and 100 represents boiling.

CHAMFER—To cut a furrow or a groove.

CHOLESTEROL—A waxy substance in animal tissue and blood.

CHROMOSOMES—The elongated bodies in the nucleus of a cell which contains the genes.

CHRONIC—Marked by long duration or frequent recurrence.

CIRCULATORY—The bodily system which contains the blood.

CIRCUMFERENCE—The outer edge enclosing an area.

CIVIC—Relating to citizenship.

CIVICS—One of the social studies focusing on government and the rights and duties of citizens.

CIVILIZATIONS—Organizations of people banded together for government, safety, worship, culture and other reasons.

CLASSICAL—Generally referring to arts or sciences prior to modern times.

CLASSIFICATION—Putting things into categories based on their likenesses.

CLAUSES—A group of words having a subject and a predicate, but only part of a complex or compound sentence.

COHERENCE—Sticking together.

COLLAGE—An art form which combines the use of two- and three-dimensional processes.

COLLECTIVE—A cooperative unit.

COLLEGIATIVE—Referring to something performed by colleagues.

COLLOQUIAL—Language use typical of a certain region.

COLONIALISM—The overseeing and governing of one country by another.

COLONIZATION—The settling (homesteading) of one country by the citizens of another.

COMBUSTION—Flaming up.

COMMA—A form of punctuation indicating a pause.

COMMENTARY—An offered opinion on something specific.

COMMODITIES—Products.

COMMUNICABLE—Able to be passed on.

COMMUNISM—A way of organizing society based on the theory that the means of production belong to the state.

COMMUTATIVE—A property of addition and multiplication saying that 3 plus 2 is the same as 2 plus 3, and 5 times 6 is the same as 6 times 5.

COMPASS—In geometry, a device used for making circles.

COMPLEX—Not simple.

COMPONENTS—Parts making up an object.

COMPOSITE—The result of putting individual parts together.

COMPOSITION—A piece of original writing.

COMPOUND—A chemical mixture. Something consisting of more than one part or substance.

COMPREHENDING—Understanding.

COMPROMISE—Give and take so an amicable solution can be reached.

COMPUTATION—The processes used in solving math problems.

CONCEPT—Idea.

CONCEPTION—The fertilization of an egg by a sperm.

CONCERTO—In music, a piece for solo instruments and orchestra.

CONCILIATION—Peacemaking.

CONCISELY—Briefly.

CONCLUSIONS—Ends. Finishes.

CONDENSATION—The process by which a gas becomes a liquid.

CONDITIONAL—Based upon circumstances.

CONDUCTORS—Substances which permit the flow of electricity or heat.

CONFEDERATION—A group of individuals or individual states banding together for a specific purpose or set of purposes.

CONGENITAL—Dating from birth but usually not hereditary.

CONGLOMERATES—Made up of parts from various sources.

CONGRUENT—Correspondence between things.

CONIC—Made up of cones; cone-like.

CONJUGATE—An arrangement of the forms of a verb.

CONJUNCTIONS—Words used to connect other words, i.e. and, but, or, nor.

CONNOTATION—A suggestive meaning.

CONSENSUS—An agreed-upon opinion.

CONSERVATISM—A philosophy of government and economics which tends to favor individualism and as little government as possible while maintaining order.

CONSONANT—In harmony; compatible.

CONSTELLATIONS—Groupings of stars in the heavens.

CONSTITUTION—A basic document containing the law of the land.

CONTEMPORARY—Of the same time.

CONTOUR—Shape.

CONTRACEPTION—Referring to devices used to prevent pregnancy.

CONVERSANT—Familiar with.

CONVERSION—Change.

CONVERT—A person who has changed from one set of beliefs to another.

COORDINATES—Sets of numbers used to specify a point in space or on a plane.

COPING—A kind of saw.

CORE—Center.

CORRELATING—Matching.

COSMIC—Referring to the heavens.

COUNTERVAILING—An opposite force.

COVERAGE—The act of covering or watching.
CRESCENDO—Increasing loudness in music.
CRITIQUE—An evaluation.
CRUST—Referring to the surface of the earth.
CUBES—A solid with six equal sides.
CUISINE—A style of cooking.
CURRICULUM—A course of study.
CURSIVE—A style of writing in which the letters are joined.
CYCLES—Series of events which repeat themselves.
CYLINDERS—Solids created by rolling up a rectangle.

D

DADO—A joint in carpentry.
DC—Direct current.
DEBUG—Get the errors out of a computer program.
DECADE—Ten years.
DECIBELS—A unit expressing the measurement of sound.
DECIMALS—A mathematical system based on tens.
DECLARATION OF INDEPENDENCE—The document declaring America's intention of separating from England.
DECLARATIVE—A sentence in the form of a statement.
DECODING—Solving.
DECOMPOSES—Breaks down.
DECRESCENDO—In music, gradually becomes softer.
DEDUCTIVE—Referring to reasoning which depends on previously known facts.
DEFERRALS—Postponements.
DEFICITS—Missing amounts.
DEGREE—Extent.
DEMISE—End. Death.
DEMOCRACY—Government of the people depending on the votes of the majority.
DENOMINATOR—The number below the line in a fraction.
DENOTATION—To indicate plainly.
DEPRECIATION—To lessen in price or value.
DEPRESSION—A time of economic slowdown and high unemployment.
DERIVATIONS—Formation of a word from an earlier root word.
DESALINIZATION—Removal of salt from water.
DETERMINANTS—Hereditary factors.
DEXTERITY—Ability to move and perform tasks easily.
DIABETES—A disease resulting from too little insulin in the blood and the inability to digest sugar.
DIAGRAMS—Drawings or models explaining something.
DIALOGUE—A discussion.
DIAMETER—A straight line drawn through the center of a circle and cutting it in half.

DICTATION—To speak or read to a person who will write or transcribe the message.

DICTIONARY—A book which defines and gives the pronunciation and spelling of words listed in alphabetical order.

DIETETICS—Science of applying nutritional principles to diet.

DIFFERENTIATION—A process by which things change.

DIGESTIVE—Referring to how living things use food.

DIGIT—A single numeral.

DILATION—Expansion.

DIMENSIONS—Measurements.

DISCERNMENT—Distinguishing things from one another.

DISCOUNTING—A deduction.

DISCRIMINATION—Ability to judge.

DISSECTING—Cutting open for examination.

DISSOLVING—Passing into a solution.

DISTORTION—Twisted out of the normal or usual.

DISTRIBUTIVE—A mathematical principle of distribution.

DIVERSIFIED—Various in form.

DNA—An acid of the nucleus which is a basis of heredity.

DOCTRINE—Something which is taught or claimed as a tenet.

DOMAIN—A sphere of influence or action.

DOMESTIC—Devoted to home duties and pleasures.

DOMINANT—Overriding; controlling.

DRAFTING—Precise drawing.

DRILL—A tool used in carpentry.

DURATION—A period of time.

E

EASEL—A prop for holding a painter's work in progress.

EBONY—A hard, black wood.

ECLIPSE—To blot out or cover.

ECOLOGY—The interaction of living things and their environments.

ECONOMICS—The study of the means of production and how products are obtained, distributed and used.

ECOSYSTEM—The combination of a community and its environment.

ELASTICITY—Stretchability.

ELECTIVE—A course of study which is not part of the required curriculum.

ELECTRICITY—Power used to move things.

ELECTROMAGNETIC—Power produced by magnets and electrons.

ELECTRON—A negatively charged particle outside of the nucleus.

ELEMENTS—Distinct parts. In chemistry, the smallest combination of molecules which makes up a particular substance.

ELEVATIONS—Drawings of things displaying three dimensions.

ELLIPSE—A closed curve with an oval shape.

EMBRYONIC—The earliest stages of the development of a fetus.

EMBRYOS—Fertilized eggs in the process of developing.

EMISSIONS—Something given off.

ENCODING—To convert a message into a coded form.

ENDOCRINE—Glands which secrete useful, necessary substances into the bloodstream.

ENERGETICS—Vigerous exercises.

ENHANCE—Improve.

ENSEMBLE—A group, usually a group producing music.

ENTERPRISE—An undertaking; a business organization.

ENVIRONMENT—Surroundings.

ENZYMES—Secretions in the body which help digest food.

EQUATION—A mathematical statement in which both sides of an example are of equal value.

EQUATORIAL—The area of the earth which is near or on the imaginary line (the equator) drawn around the earth's center.

EQUILIBRIUM—Evenness. In balance.

EQUIVALENT—Just about equal to.

EROSION—Breaking down or wearing away, especially of soil.

ESSAY—Written commentary on a topic.

ESTIMATING—Judging.

ESTIMATION—In mathematics, coming close to a correct answer.

ETCHING—A drawing produced with the use of acid.

ETHNIC—Referring to a particular culture.

ETYMOLOGY—Study of the history of words.

EVALUATE—Judge. Rate. Place a value on.

EVAPORATION—The process by which a liquid becomes a gas.

EVOLUTION—A theory that states that living things have evolved from simpler to more complex forms.

EXCHANGE—Give something in order to get something else.

EXCLAMATORY—A sentence form used to show high emotion.

EXCRETORY—A bodily system which processes and removes waste.

EXPANSIONS—Growths.

EXPLOITS—Adventures.

EXPONENTS—Small numerals used to indicate the number of times a number is to be multiplied by itself.

EXPOSED—Uncovered.

EXPOSITORY—A type of writing, the purpose of which is to provide information.

EXTINCTION—Killing off.

EXTRACTING—Pulling forth.

F

FABLES—Stories intended to teach a lesson.

FACILITY—A place used for a particular purpose.

FACTOR—A mathematical term used to identify a part of a multiplication process.

FACTORING—Identifying all the possible factors.

FAHRENHEIT—A scale for measuring temperature in which 32 degrees is freezing and 212 degrees is boiling.

FASCISM—A political philosophy which is racist and advocates dictatorship and oppression.

FEDERALISTS—People who support a government in which individual states give up part of their power to a central entity.

FERROUS—Made up of or containing large quantities of iron.

FERTILIZATION—The process by which a sperm and an egg combine.

FEUDALISM—A way of organizing a society so that there are overlords who own serfs (servants) and offer them protection in return for labor.

FIGURATIVE—Not completely exact. Used as the opposite of literal.

FILTERS—Screens out.

FISSION—Breaking apart.

FIXATIFS—Substances sprayed onto surfaces to keep chalks from rubbing off.

FLUENT—Used with reference to language meaning very well able to use it properly and understand it.

FOCUS—To center in on.

FOOTNOTING—Adding some words of explanation or reference at the bottom of a written page.

FORMATTED—Put into a particular form.

FORMULAS—A statement used to express a rule or a truth.

FOSSIL—A preserved impression of the remains of a plant or animal from ages past.

FRACTIONS—Parts of a quantity.

FRAGMENTS—Bits or pieces.

FREQUENCY—Referring to a radio wave signal.

FRICTION—Rubbing of one body against another.

FUNCTIONS—Ways of behaving.

FUNDAMENTAL—Very basic.

FUNGI—A kind of plant life which has no chlorophyll and is therefore dependent on other plants for survival.

FUSION—A melding together.

G

GALL—Anger or annoy; also bile produced by the liver.

GALLAXIES—Masses of stars and planets in the universe.

GALVANIC—Electricity produced by a chemical reaction.

GEARS—Toothed wheels which interlock with other toothed wheels.

GENDER—Sex.

GENES—Units in a chromosome which are carriers of heredity.

GENETIC—Referring to the genes responsible for heredity.

GEOLOGICAL—Referring to the science of the history of the earth.

GEOMETRIC—Referring to the study of geometry or to figures which are used in geometry (squares, circles, triangles, etc.).

GERMS—Disease-causing microscopic entities.

GERUNDS—Words which have the characteristics of both nouns and verbs.

GLANDS—A group of cells in a body which secrete specific substances.

GLOBAL—Earth-wide.

GNP—Gross national product; an economic measure.

GRAINS—Tiny particles.

GRAMMATICAL—In conformance with the rules of grammar.

GRAVITATIONAL—The pull of the force of gravity.

GROOMING—Caring for one's body.

GYRATION—Twisting and turning.

H

HARMONIC—A pleasing agreement of sounds.

HEMISPHERE—Half of a sphere; half of the globe.

HEREDITY—The passing on of traits from one generation to another.

HERITAGE—The traits and traditions one inherits from previous generations.

HETERO—Differing.

HOMOGRAPHS—Two or more words spelled alike but with different meanings (read, read).

HOMONYMS—Homographs.

HOMOPHONES—Homographs.

HONED—Sharpened.

HORIZONTAL—Across, like the horizon.

HUMANITIES—Branches of learning accenting the cultural.

HYBRID—A mixture of traits resulting in an individual differing from its parent.

HYDROCARBONS—An organic compound containing only hydrogen and carbon.

HYDROSTATIC—Liquids at rest.

HYPOTHESES—Statements of prediction.

I

IDIOMS—Expressions peculiar to a language which cannot be translated word for word.

ILLUSTRATE—Picture. Give an example.

IMAGERY—The products of imagination.

IMMIGRATION—Entering and taking up residence in a foreign country.

IMPERIALISM—Seeking power over other countries.

IMPLICATIONS—Hints or suggestions rather than direct statements

INCEPTION—From the beginning.

INDEX—An alphabetical list of items.

INDUCTION—Reasoning from a part to a whole.

INDUSTRIAL—Having to do with large businesses.

INEQUALITIES—The opposite of equations; things which are unequal.

INERTIA—A property of matter at rest.

INFERENCE—A guess or a deduction.

INFINITE—Without beginning or end.

INFINITIVE—A verb form having the characteristics of both a noun and a verb and usually used with "to."

INFLATION—A period in which prices rise and the value of money falls.

INGESTION—Eating.

INORGANIC—Not plant or animal; mineral.

INSIGHT—Understanding; ability to see into a situation.

INSPIRATION—A new or original idea.

INSTILL—To impart or cause to enter.

INSULATORS—Materials which will not conduct electricity or heat.

INTAGLIO—An engraving on a hard surface.

INTEGERS—Whole numbers which do not include fractions.

INTEGRAL—A vital or central part of.

INTEGRATED—Mixed.

INTEGRITY—Adherence to a code of ethics.

INTELLIGIBLY—Able to be understood.

INTENSITY—Strength; energy; force.

INTERCEPT—Come between and stop forward motion.

INTERDEPENDENCE—Reliance on one another.

INTERJECTIONS—Exclamatory words (ouch, hah, stop, etc.)

INTERROGATIVE—Questioning.

INTERSECTIONS—Points at which things (especially lines or roads) come together and cross each other.

INTERVALS—Spaces.

INTONATION—The pattern of rise and fall of the voice in speech.

INVERSION—Turning something upside down.

INVESTIGATE—Study; look into.

IRRATIONAL—Not reasonable.

ISOBAR—A line on a map connecting places which have equal barometric pressure.

ISOLATED—All alone.

ISOMETRIC—A series of exercises involving force and counterforce.

ISOTHERMAL—Equality of temperature.

ISOTOPES—Atoms which are nearly identical but differ in the number of neutrons.

K

KEYBOARDING—Using the keyboard of a computer.

KILN—A very hot oven used for hardening ceramics.

KILOGRAM—A unit of weight in the metric system.

KILOMETER—A unit of distance in the metric system.

KINEMATICS—A science which deals with motion apart from mass or force.

KINETIC—The force and energy of material bodies and their motion.

L

LASERS—Instruments which focus intense beams of light.

LATERAL—Sideways.

LATHE—A machine which turns objects so they can be easily and evenly carved.

LATITUDE—A set of imaginary lines parallel to the equator and going from pole to pole.

LEAGUE—A group of like-minded individuals.

LEDGER—A notebook used for keeping business accounts.

LEGACIES—Inheritances.

LEGENDS—Stories told from one generation to another over many years.

LEVERS—Instruments used for prying or lifting.

LIBERALISM—A political philosophy which generally looks to government to right social wrongs.

LINEAR—Referring to a straight line.

LITER—A measure of volume in the metric system.

LITERATURE—The art of using the written word to express emotion, information and beauty.

LONGITUDE—A set of imaginary lines belting the earth and passing through both the north and south poles.

M

MACRAME—An art form based on tying knots.

MAGNETISM—A quality of attraction like that of a magnet for iron.

MANIPULATE—Move about in response to one's will.

MANTLE—The earth's covering.

MANUSCRIPT—A written document which has not been published; a type of handwriting in which the letters are not joined.

MASS—A quality of matter.

MATTING—A border used for a picture prior to framing it.

MATURATION—Growth.

MEAN—Average.

MEDIA—Those things which the artist used to create; also used to refer to the means of mass communication.

METABOLISM—The processes by which substances are handled by the body.

METALURGY—The science and technology of metals.

METAPHOR—A word used in place of another to create an image and suggest likeness between them. (The ship plows the sea.)

METEOROLOGY—Weather forecasting.

METERS—Measuring devices.

METHODOLOGY—A way of doing things.

METRIC—A system of measurement.

MICROORGANISMS—Plant and animal life too small to be seen by the naked eye which can be seen under a microscope.

MEDIEVAL—Referring to the historical period known as the Middle Ages; from about 500 to 1500 A.D.

MIGRATIONS—Movements of large groups.

MINORITIES—People who differ in some way from those who make up the majority.

MINUEND—Top number in a subtraction example.

MITER—Cut a specific angle.

MODELING—Sculpting; also serving as an example.

MODEMS—Devices for communicating between a computer and a data bank.

MODIFIERS—Things which limit the meaning.

MOLECULES—The smallest particle of matter which is chemically the same as the whole.

MOMENTUM—The force of a body.

MONARCHIES—Kingdoms.

MONO—Single or one.

MONOPHONIC—A single-transmission path of sound.

MONOPOLY—Exclusive ownership.

MORES—A set of cultural behaviors of a group.

MORTISES—Holes cut into pieces of wood to form a joint.

MULTIPLE—Many.

MULTITUDE—A great many people.

MURAL—A wall painting.

MUTATION—Change; usually with reference to a change in a living thing.

MYTHOLOGY—A body of tales usually dealing with gods and heroes.

N

NARRATIVES—Long tales.

NATAL—Referring to birth.

NATIONALISM—A philosophy binding a people to a country.

NEWTONIAN—Referring to classical physics.

NOMENCLATURE—Naming.

NOTATION—In music, the written form of music.

NOUN—The name of a person, place or thing.

NUCLEAR—Referring to the nucleus of a cell.

NUCLEUS—The part of a cell containing the genes and chromosomes; the core or central mass.

NUMBER—Quantity.

NUMERAL—The written symbol used to indicate a number.

NURTURING—Feeding and caring for.

NUTRITION—Food.

O

OBESITY—Overweight.

OCEANOGRAPHY—The science of oceans and their phenomena.

OCTAVES—Eight note spans.

OFFICIATING—Acting in an official capacity.

OMNIVORES—Animals which eat both plants and animals.

OPERA—Drama set to music.

OPTIONS—Choices.

ORBIT—The path one body takes in its revolution about another.

ORDERING—In mathematics, putting numbers in a particular ranking order.

ORDINAL—As distinct from cardinal with reference to numbers; first, second, third, fourth, etc.

ORGANIC—Dealing with carbon compounds.

ORGANISM—A living thing.

ORTHOGRAPHIC—Relating to spelling.

OSCILLATIONS—Vibrations.

OXIDATION—Combining with oxygen.

P

PALSY—A condition marked by tremors.

PAPIER-MACHE—A combination of paper and flour used in sculpture.

PARABOLA—A curve formed by the intersection of a cone and a plane.

PARADOX—A statement which is probably true but is contrary to common sense.

PARAGRAPHS—A subdivision of a written composition containing one or more sentences.

PARALLELISM—Agreement of a subject and predicate in a sentence.

PARAMECIA—Certain one-celled animals.

PARAPHRASE—Explain or rephrase.

PARITY—On a par or equal with.

PARLIAMENTARY—According to a formal set of rules.

PARTICIPLES—Words having the characteristics of both a verb and an adjective.

PARTICLES—Very small bits of matter.

PASTELS—Pale or light colors.

PATINA—Green film formed on brass and copper.

PATRIOTIC—Love of country.

PEDESTALS—Raised columns.

PEERS—Those of the same age or group.

PENTAGONS—Five-sided structures.

PERCENTAGE—A part of something larger.

PERIMETER—The encircling outer edge.

PERIODIC—Occurring at regular time intervals.

PERPENDICULAR—Meeting another line at right angles.

PERSPECTIVE—Painting and drawing with depth and distance.

PHASES—Stages or intervals.

PHONICS—A method of learning to read by sounding out letters and letter combinations.

PHOTOSYNTHESIS—The process plants use to combine sunlight and water and create sugar.

PHRASE—A brief expression in words.

PHYSICS—The study of the physical environment and how it works.

PICTOGRAPHS—Prehistoric drawings on a rock wall.

PITCH—In music, the highness or lowness of sound.

PLANES—Level or flat surfaces (two dimensional).

PLATEN—The paper roller on a typewriter.

PLATES—In geology, the surfaces the continents ride on.

PLURAL—More than one.

POLAR—Referring to matters having a relationship to the north or south pole; also positive or negative poles in electricity.

POLITICS—The art or practice of getting into and staying in government.

POLYGONS—Multi-sided structures.

POLYNOMIAL—An expression in Algebra which has two or more terms.

POLYPHONIC—In music, having two or more harmonious parts.

PORTFOLIO—A portable case for papers or artwork.

POSSESSIVES—Parts of speech indicating belonging.

POSTULATES—Statements presumed to be true.

POSTURE—A manner of carrying one's body.

PRECIS—A shortening of a written work containing its essential points and meanings.

PREDICATE—The part of a sentence which tells about the subject.

PREFIXES—A combination of letters (affix) occurring at the beginning of a word.

PREHISTORIC—Before written history.

PREPOSITION—A word which combines with a noun or pronoun to form a phrase.

PREPRIMER—A very simple, very early reader with only a few words which are frequently repeated.

PRIMARY—Very early and very basic.

PRIMITIVE—Related to a very early stage of development.

PRIME—Not capable of being divided evenly by any number except itself and one.

PRIMER—A basic reader ordinarily used in the first grade.

PRISM—A three-sided glass or crystal that breaks up light into a rainbow of colors.

PROBABILITY—Having a likelihood of being true.

PROBE—Investigate.

PROFICIENCY—Ability.

PROGRESSIVE—Advancing by stages.

PROJECTION—Causing light or shadow to fall on a surface.

PRONOUNS—Words which stand in place of a noun such as he, she, it, etc.

PROOFREADING—Reading a document for the purpose of finding and correcting errors.

PROOFS—Trial runs; in math, recalculations.

PROPAGANDA—Spread of information to further a cause.

PROPAGATION—Breeding.

PROPORTION—Size relationship.

PROPRIETORSHIP—Ownership.

PROSE—The ordinary language of people in speaking or writing.

PROTIST—A single-celled organism.

PROTRACTOR—An instrument used for constructing and measuring angles.

PROVE—Show to be correct or true.

PSYCHOLOGY—The science of investigating the mind and emotions.

PULLEYS—Wheels with one or more grooves used for hoisting.

PUNCTUATION—Inserting standardized marks into writing to clarify meanings.

PYRAMID—A structure with a polygon base and triangular sides meeting at a point.

Q

QUACKERY—Pretense of medical skill.

QUADRATIC—Four-sided.

QUADRILATERALS—Flat structures with four sides.

QUANTUM—An elemental unit of energy.

QUARK—Elementary particle.

QUOTATION MARK—One of a pair of punctuation marks used to indicate what a person is saying.

R

RABBET—A grove in a joint made to have another piece inserted.

RACISM—Prejudice against people of another race.

RADIAN—Unit of angular measurement in a circle.

RADIATION—Spreading of rays from a central point.

RADICAL—A person who favors rapid and sweeping change.

RADICALS—Roots in mathematics; atoms which remain at rest during chemical reactions.

RADIOACTIVITY—Emission of rays as the nucleus of certain atoms disintegrate.

RADIUS—A straight line extending from the center of a circle to its circumference.

RANGE—Distance.

RATIO—Relationship between sets of numbers.

RATIONAL—Sane; reasonable.

RAYS—Beams.

REBUS—Representation of words by drawing pictures.

RECESSION—A period of slowed-down economic activity.

RECESSIVE—Quality of a gene carrying a trait that doesn't show if a dominant gene is paired with it.

RECITALS—Performances, generally by students.

RECONSTRUCTION—Rebuilding; also the period in American history right after the Civil War.

RECTANGLE—Flat structure with four sides and four equal angles.

REDUCE—Diminish; in math, bring to its lowest form.

REFLECTION—Light heat or sound bouncing off a surface and back toward its source.

REFORMATION—A period in history when profound religious changes took place.

REFRACTION—The bending of a ray of light, heat or sound.

RELATIVITY—Einstein's theory concerning mass and energy.

RELIEF—Three-dimensional art on a two-dimensional surface.

REMAINDER—The fractional quantity left over in a division example.

RENAISSANCE—That historical period after the Dark Ages during which there was a notable rebirth of interest in culture and the arts.

REPRODUCTION—In biology, the process of having babies.

REPULSION—Pushing away; rejecting.

RESISTORS—In electricity, devices used to slow down or stop the flow of current.

RESONANCE—Prolonged or increased sound.

RESPIRATION—Breathing.

REVOLUTION—An internal war within a country.

RHYTHM—Regular rise and fall in the flow of movement or sound.

RIVETING—Holding. Joining with rivets.

RNA—Ultimate genetic material along with DNA in the chromosomes.

ROBOTIC—Having to do with robots.

ROTATIONS—Turnings.

ROUNDING—Estimating to a nearest convenient number.

S

SATIRE—Biting wit; irony or sarcasm.

SCULPTURE—Three-dimensional art.

SECTORS—Parts of a circle or parts of a region.

SEDIMENT—Material which settles to the bottom of a liquid.

SEGMENTS—Parts; sections.

SEMESTER—Half of a school year; a term.

SEQUENCE—Order.

SHADES—Colors or tints.

SILVERPOINT—A type of pencil used in producing finely drawn lines.

SIMILE—A figure of speech comparing two unlike things, e.g. legs like tree trunks.

SIMPLIFYING—Making less complicated.

SIMULATION—Creation of the appearance of.

SKELETAL—Referring to the bones.

SKIM—Read very quickly, not stopping at each word.

SLAB—A thick, flat surface.

SLIDES—Pieces of cut glass used for mounting specimens for examination under a microscope.

SLOPE—Ground which forms an incline.

SOCIALISM—Government based on state ownership of property and distribution of goods and services.

SOCIOLOGY—Social science based on study of interrelationships.

SOFTWARE—Computer programs.

SOLAR—Having to do with the sun.

SOLDERING—Joining by means of heat and a melted soft metal.

SOLUBILITY—Able to be dissolved in a liquid.

SOLUTIONS—Mixtures of liquids.

SOLVENTS—Chemicals which dissolve other chemicals.

SONAR—Focusing and bouncing back of sound waves.

SONNETS—Poems having a prescribed structure.

SPATIAL—Referring to space.

SPECTRAL—Ghostly.

SPHERE—A ball or globe.

SPLINES—Slats.

SQUARE—Flat structure with four equal sides.

SQUARING—Multiplying a number by itself.

STATIC—In place; unmoving. In music, an interfering sound.

STATISTICS—Data collected and arranged in an orderly way.

STELLAR—Referring to stars.

STOICHIOMETRY—The branch of sciences and equal angles.

STRUCTURE—Form or format.

SUBJECT—The person, place or thing which a sentence tells about.

SUBORDINATION—Placement in a lower rank or class.

SUBSTANCE—Mass. Essential part.

SUBTRACTION—Taking one quantity away from another.

SUFFIXES—Affixes added to the end of a word.

SUMMARIES—Brief coverings of the main points.

SUMS—Totals. The result of adding numbers together.

SYMBOL—Something used to represent something else.

SYMMETRY—Evenness, Likeness, Correspondence.

SYMPHONY—A complex composition for a full orchestra.

SYMBIOSIS—Two different organisms living together benefitting both.

SYNCOPATION—Accenting notes on the weak beat.

SYNONYMS—Words which have the same or very similar meanings.

SYNTHETIC—Man-made, Artificial.

T

TANGENT—A plane which touches but does not cut into the circumference of a circle.

TECHNIQUES—Methods.

TECHNOLOGICAL — Techniques used to deal with machinery and electronics.
TECTONICS — The geological study of movement of the earth's plates.
TEMPO — Timing
TEMPRA — An egg-based, watercolor paint.
TENONS — Parts of joints in carpentry.
TENSES — Referring to verbs and indicating time.
TEXTURE — The visual and tactile surface of objects.
THEMES — Essays or compositions.
THEOREM — A statement in mathematics which has been or is to be proven.
THEORETICAL — Pertaining to theories.
THEORY — A general principle presumed to be true.
THERMODYNAMICS — Physics that deals with heat.
TIMBRE — The distinctive quality of a sound.
TINTS — Colors lightly.
TONGUE — An appendage in a mouth or in a shoe.
TOPOGRAPHIC — Showing, on a map, the physical features of a location.
TOTALITARIANISM — Governmental philosophy holding that the individual is totally subordinate to the state.
TRANSCENDENTALISM — Philosophy holding that the ultimate reality is unknowable.
TRANSCRIBING — Changing written notes from one form to another.
TRANSFORMERS — Devices which alter electric current.
TRANSISTORS — A small electronic semiconductor.
TRANSITION — An interim stage; going from one stage to another.
TRANSMUTATIONS — Changes or alterations in form.
TRANSPOSE — In music, to write in a different key.
TRAPEZOID — A four-sided structure with two parallel sides.
TRIANGLES — A structure having three sides and three internal angles.
TRIGONOMETRIC — Related to the mathematical study of trigonometry.

U

UNIVERSE — Entire sweep of the heavens including everything.
URBANIZATION — Becoming like a city.
UTOPIANISM — Ideal living conditions.

V

VARIABLES — Things which are subject to change.
VARIATION — Change.
VASCULAR — Relating to the bodily channels which conduct fluid in plants or animals.
VECTOR — A quantity which has size and direction.
VELOCITY — Speed.
VENEREAL — Related to sexual intercourse.

VERB—A word which expresses an act, an occurrence or a state of being.

VERBAL—Able to express oneself.

VERTICAL—Straight up or down.

VIRUSES—A disease-producing agent too small to be seen by microscopes and usually without a nucleus.

VOCABULARY—The use of words.

VOCAL—Referring to the voice and ability to produce sound.

VOLUME—The amount of bulk; the degree of loudness of sound.

W

WAVES—Up-and-down movements of liquids, sounds, light and air.

WEBS—Networks of threads mostly spun by spiders.

WOODWINDS—Instruments of an orchestra including oboes, clarinets, English horns, flutes, etc.

Y

YEAST—Cells of a microscopic fungus which by multiplying causes dough to rise and fruits to ferment.

YOGA—A form of exercise and meditation based on an Eastern philosophy.

Z

ZERO—The identity element for addition and subtraction.

ZOOLOGY—The study of animal life forms.